CYBERSAFETY

Information Crisis

CYBERSAFETY

CYBERSAFETY

Information Crisis

MICHAEL LOSAVIO

CONSULTING EDITOR

MARCUS K. ROGERS, Ph.D., CISSP, DFCP

Founder and Director,
Cyber Forensics Program,
Purdue University

  CHELSEA HOUSE
An Infobase Learning Company

Cybersafety: Information Crisis

Copyright © 2012 by Infobase Learning

Chelsea House
An Infobase Learning Company
132 West 31st Street
New York NY 10001

Library of Congress Cataloging-in-Publication Data
Losavio, Michael.
    Information crisis / Michael Losavio ; consulting editor, Marcus K. Roger.
        p. cm. — (Cybersafety)
    Includes bibliographical references and index.
    ISBN-13: 978-1-60413-701-9 (acid-free paper)
    ISBN-10: 1-60413-701-0 (acid-free paper) 1. Computer network resources—Evaluation.
2. Web sites—Evaluation. 3. Electronic information resource literacy. 4. Internet research.
5. Internet fraud. 6. Internet—Safety measures. I. Rogers, Marcus K. II. Title. III. Series.
    ZA4150.L67 2011
    025.042'5—dc23
                            2011029186

Chelsea House books are available at special discounts when purchased in bulk quantities for businesses, associations, institutions, or sales promotions. Please call our Special Sales Department in New York at (212) 967-8800 or (800) 322-8755.

You can find Chelsea House on the World Wide Web at http://www.infobasepublishing.com

Text design by Erik Lindstrom
Cover design by Takeshi Takahashi
Composition by EJB Publishing Services
Cover printed by Yurchak Printing, Landisville, Pa.
Book printed and bound by Yurchak Printing, Landisville, Pa.

Printed in the United States of America

This book is printed on acid-free paper.

All links and Web addresses were checked and verified to be correct at the time of publication. Because of the dynamic nature of the Web, some addresses and links may have changed since publication and may no longer be valid.

CONTENTS

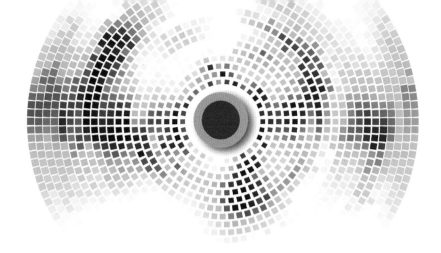

Foreword

The Internet has had and will continue to have a profound effect on society. It is hard to imagine life without such technologies as computers, cell phones, gaming devices, and so on. The Internet, World Wide Web, and their associated technologies have altered our social and personal experience of the world. In no other time in history have we had such access to knowledge and raw information. One can search the Library of Congress, the Louvre in Paris, and read online books and articles or watch videos from just about any country in the world. We can interact and chat with friends down the street, in another state, or half way around the globe. The world is now our neighborhood. We are a "wired" society who lives a significant amount of our life online and tethered to technology.

The Internet, or cyberspace, is a great enabler. What is also becoming apparent, though, is that there is a dark side to this global wired society. As the concept of who our friends are moves from real world relationships to cyberspace connections, so also do the rules change regarding social conventions and norms. How many friends do we have online that we have actually met in person? Are online-only friends even real or at the very least whom they claim to be? We also begin to redefine privacy. Questions arise over what should be considered private or public information. Do we really want everyone in the global society to have access to our personal information? As with the real world there may be people online that we do not wish to associate with or grant access to our lives.

It is easy to become enamored with technology and the technology/information revolution. It is equally as easy to become paranoid about the dangers inherent in cyberspace. What is difficult but necessary is to be realistic about how our world has been forever changed. We see numerous magazine, TV, and newspaper headlines regarding the latest cybercrime attacks. Stories about identity theft being the fastest growing non-violent criminal activity are common. The government is concerned with cyber or information warfare attacks against critical infrastructures. Given this kind of media coverage it is easy to think that the sky is falling and cyberspace is somehow evil. Yet if we step back and think about it, technology is neither good nor bad, it simply *is*. Technology is neutral; it is what we do with technology that determines whether it improves our lives or damages and makes our lives more difficult. Even if someone is on the proverbial fence over whether the Internet and cyberspace are society enablers or disablers, what is certain is that the technology genie is out of the bottle. We will never be able to put it back in; we need to learn how to master and live with it.

Learning to live with the Internet and its technological offshoots is one of the objectives behind the Cybersafety series of books. The immortal words of Sir Francis Bacon (the father of the scientific method) "knowledge is power" ring especially true today. If we live in a society that is dependent on technology and therefore we live a significant portion of our daily lives in cyberspace, then we need to understand the potential downside as well as the upside. However, what is not useful is fear mongering or the demonization of technology.

There is no doubt that cyberspace has its share of bad actors and criminals. This should not come as a surprise to anyone. Cyberspace mirrors traditional society, including both the good and unfortunately the bad. Historically criminals have been attracted to new technologies in an effort to improve and extend their criminal methods. The same advantages that technology and cyberspace bring to our normal everyday lives (e.g., increased communication, the ability to remotely access information) can be used in a criminal manner. Online fraud, identity theft, cyberstalking, and cyberbullying are but a few of the ugly behaviors that we see online today.

Navigating successfully through cyberspace also means that we need to understand how the "cyber" affects our personality and social behavior. One of the empowering facets of cyberspace and technology is the fact that we can escape reality and find creative outlets for ourselves. We can immerse ourselves in computer and online games, and if so inclined, satisfy our desire to gamble or engage in other risky behaviors. The sense of anonymity and the ability to redefine who we are online can be intoxicating to some people. We can experiment with new roles and behaviors that may be polar opposites of who we are in the real physical world. Yet, as in the real world, our activities and behaviors in cyberspace have consequences too. Well-meaning escapism can turn to online addictions; seemingly harmless distractions like online gaming can consume so much of our time that our real world relationships and lives are negatively affected. The presumed anonymity afforded by cyberspace can lead to bullying and stalking, behaviors that can have a profound and damaging impact on the victims and on ourselves.

The philosophy behind the Cybersafety series is based on the recognition that cyberspace and technology will continue to play an increasingly important part of our everyday lives. The way in which we define who we are, our home life, school, social relationships, and work life will all be influenced and impacted by our online behaviors and misbehaviors. Our historical notions of privacy will also be redefined in terms of universal access to our everyday activities and posted musings. The Cybersafety series was created to assist us in understanding and making sense of the online world. The intended audience for the series is those individuals who are and will be the most directly affected by cyberspace and its technologies, namely young people (i.e., those in grades 6–12).

Young people are the future of our society. It is they who will go forward and shape societal norms, customs, public policy, draft new laws, and be our leaders. They will be tasked with developing positive coping mechanisms for both the physical and cyberworlds. They will have dual citizenship responsibilities: citizens of the physical and of the cyber. It is hoped that this series will assist in providing insight, guidance, and positive advice for this journey.

The series is divided into books that logically gather related concepts and issues. The goal of each book in the series is not to scare but to educate and inform the reader. As the title of the series states the focus is on "safety." Each book in the series provides advice on what to watch out for and how to be safer. The emphasis is on education and awareness while providing a frank discussion related to the consequences of certain online behaviors.

It is my sincere pleasure and honor to be associated with this series. As a former law enforcement officer and current educator, I am all too aware of the dangers that can befall our young people. I am also keenly aware that young people are more astute than some adults commonly give them credit for being. Therefore it is imperative that we begin a dialogue that enhances our awareness and encourages and challenges the reader to reexamine their behaviors and attitudes toward cyberspace and technology. We fear what we do not understand; fear is not productive, but knowledge is empowering. So let's begin our collective journey into arming ourselves with more knowledge.

—Marcus K. Rogers, Ph. D., CISSP, DFCP,
Founder and Director,
Cyber Forensics Program,
Purdue University

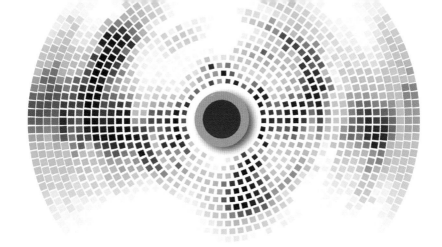

Introduction

Things have really changed.

Everyone now has easy access to a great deal of information. Even just a few years ago, most information was controlled and reviewed by others before it reached the public, but not anymore. With the rise of the Internet, its global expansion, and the ease of access available through mobile computing devices, it is possible to know so much more. This is the legacy of the Internet.

The Internet is a revolutionary tool for getting and giving information. It gives a person direct access to billions of pieces of information and knowledge in text, picture, sound, and video form with new ways to control that information. The information can be accessed almost anywhere at any time, using

- a library or home computer
- a personal netbook or other laptop computer
- a smartphone with voice, text, or Web service

- a seatback computer in an airplane over the Atlantic ocean
- a dashboard computer in a new car
- an iPad or similar tablet device

In exchange for that freedom and power, people now face new responsibilities. These responsibilities may never have been explained to them and may require skills that have never been taught to them. This would not be a particularly big deal if those responsibilities only dealt with minor issues. Buying a new song from a favorite artist based on online recommendations will, at worst, provide disappointment if the song is not very good. Those

iPhones and other smartphones make information accessible virtually any-where at any time. (*Imaginechina via AP Images*)

responsibilities grow into major issues, though, when people use technology to get information to make crucial, important decisions about their lives and the lives of their friends and family. For example, making a personal health decision based on an inaccurate online recommendation can lead to injury, illness, or worse. It is important for people to be aware of these risks with online information. This is particularly true because much of the talk about these new, online responsibilities is about security and safety, not necessarily the actual impact of the information people get online. *Competent and secure computer use* is important, as it often deals with how people use the Internet to communicate with others through chat rooms, Facebook, and other social media. There is a risk that a person may link up with someone they do not really know and possibly should not trust or that they may reveal sensitive, personal information. These dangers are very real and very serious.

Good, safe computer use, though, is harder to understand. It is much broader and more important. Safe computer use really means the safe and competent practice and use of that which computers and the Internet provide, which is all the wonderful information coming from Web sites, e-mail, chat rooms, social networking sites, online encyclopedias, databases, blogs, and any other online means of communication.

Secure computer use deals with operating in an environment that is free from danger or that protects against crime. Safe computer use is more about protecting against risk or being harmed through unintended consequences or misinformation.

Safe computer use can be harder to achieve than most people know.

Usually people do not lie to each other face-to-face, even when one person is trying to sell something to another. That is due, in part, to many face-to-face contacts occurring between people known and in the local community, people whose relationships require trust and honesty. A local newspaper or television news show builds viewers by providing good, trusted information. A library encyclopedia is acquired by a librarian, whose training and ethical duties require that he or she offer reliable information to the community. But online computer use takes place in a different universe of people known only to each other through information that may or may not be real. Parent or child, student or teacher, employee or employer, friend or foe, all face this new challenge posed by the reliability of information they find or are given. Online information simply is not always what it seems.

People online must determine for themselves if what they have found is good or bad information, truthful commentary, or manipulative lying. There is no longer a librarian or teacher or parent or boss or mentor to shield or guide people, young or old, from a direct encounter with new information. In many cases, there is not even an editor, publisher, guardian, or reviewer putting a stamp of approval on online information to even claim it is reliable. Each person becomes his or her own librarian/teacher/mentor. This means that each person posting information has a responsibility to assure the reliability of that information. It is a responsibility to others who need accurate information and who, out of respect for other people, no one would wish to mislead.

This book addresses this new crisis in the reliability of information now available everywhere, describes what kind of information exists on the Internet, and explains the skills a person must use to assure they have found good, reliable information online.

It is a crisis because that information is everywhere and available to everyone but with no clear signs of the dangers from bad or misleading material.

Mastering the skills to judge the reliability of information may not be easy.

Everyone must be careful. This book is about why, where, and how to be careful.

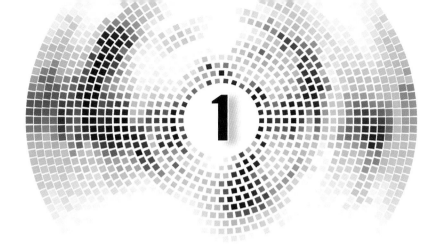

The Power of the Internet

Brittany chose to do her senior essay on health care reform. Her focus was on how to make health care more affordable for Americans. She began her research, as many people do, by using the search engine Google. After a couple of searches, she was stunned to find a table of information from a seemingly reputable source that listed all of the hospital companies in her region and the pay for the men and women who ran those companies. The table showed that those men and women were paid very well, but that the president of what appeared to be the smallest hospital was paid almost 10 percent of the total operating revenue for the hospital as his salary. This was at one of the most prominent hospitals in her city.

Brittany was outraged. She perceived this as one of the biggest reasons that health care costs had become so unreasonable. How could anybody take so much money from people who came to the hospital for medical care? This was exactly the kind of greed and abuse that was driving up health care costs.

Brittany made this table a focus of her paper, properly citing her source. She used this as clear evidence of how the business of health care had taken over from caring for people, and she expressed her outrage throughout the essay.

She turned her essay in on time and expected a good grade. So she was stunned when, a week later, she received her paper back with a grade of C-minus.

Attached to her essay was a report from the federal Department of Health and Human Services which showed that, contrary to her information, the hospital that was the focus of her essay was the largest in the region with revenues 10 times those that she used to base her argument. Relative to other hospitals and their operating managers, the salary of this hospital's president was typical and in line with that of other businesses. Her teacher's notes pointed out that her entire argument was based on bad information. Starting from a bad foundation, her arguments missed the point of the assignment, leading to her low grade. Brittany had not confirmed the information in the table against other sources or confirmed that her source for the table was accurate.

Was Brittany just an exception, a poor student who didn't know how to do her research and study properly? Or is she just one of many students who make that same mistake?

The tool called the Internet is a communication system that lets people use many different services to connect with people, information, and resources around the world. It is a network of computer networks. The part of the Internet called the World Wide Web, in which people use Web browsers like Internet Explorer and Firefox, is a system for linking people to all kinds of information that, in turn, links to other information. E-mail, video calling, and peer-to-peer, file-sharing services are other services over the Internet. Collectively, the "Internet" is considered by many to be the most powerful new information tool of the last 600 years. From the movable type printing press invented by Johannes Gutenberg around 1450 to today's electronic information technologies, the availability of knowledge to the average person has expanded tremendously. If "knowledge is power," this access lets people do amazing new things. No longer must a person ask someone else to show them how to do things. No longer must someone first find a library and then find a book and then find a chapter that describes what they need to know. Any person can get the knowledge they need from any point in the world where they are online, whether with a smart phone, tablet, notebook, computer kiosk, or other device.

A Newcastle University (England) student checks the "Bincam" Facebook page in June 2011. As of then, five households had signed up for a university program that puts photographs of every item placed in a particular garbage can on Facebook in a bid to raise consciousness about recycling efforts. (*AP Photo/Scott Heppell*)

This change can be seen in the way people exchange information with each other, including friends, family, and even complete strangers. The term *social media* applies to Internet-based systems that let people connect regardless of physical distance between them in ways that can further relationships, particularly between people who trust (or at least do not dislike) each other. Their relationships are built on information.

Online, one can find great music that never plays on the radio, listen to a preview without charge, and obtain it for a price much less than in local stores. One can find out when a car dealer may be overcharging or is offering a fair price. A person can check on the best prices in town for things they want or need: shoes, clothes, music, computers, groceries, and so on. The list is almost endless.

A person can learn about his or her own health or that of a loved one by accessing medical information online. One can find the best

THE RISE OF FACEBOOK

In 2004 students at Harvard University created an Internet Web site for sharing information about themselves with their friends. At first, the Web site was only for students at their university. Later they began to make it available to students at other universities around the United States. Over time they opened their Web site, styled "a social network," to people all over the world.

By 2011 this "social network" had more than 500 million users.

Such has been the development of Facebook, which in a short span of years has grown into an Internet service valued at as much as $50 billion.

The Internet has led to this and other new ways for people to share information about each other and their interests. With this have come controversies over the good and bad uses of such a powerful tool.

prices on medicines or anything else a family might need or want, whether a textbook or a huge LED television. A person can track crime trends and criminals in their neighborhood and take safety measures against the methods used by the criminals. People can help friends find solutions to their problems, even if they do not know the answers right away.

All of this can be done in the palm of one's hand.

It is amazing, but it comes with a price: *The truth and accuracy of information provided online and even a person's right to use that information must be verified before it is used.* The Internet and the services on it do not guarantee that. It is the responsibility of the person using it to check on the truth and accuracy of what they find.

Court cases offer some insight into legal and practical issues related to the Internet. The first Internet case in the U.S. Supreme Court, *Janet Reno, Attorney General Of The United States, et al., v. American Civil Liberties Union et al.,* 521 U.S. 844 (1997), showed how the Supreme Court appreciated the immense potential of the Internet.[1]

It came in the context of a very serious policy issue regarding the kinds of information to be allowed on the new Internet. The question was: how far can the government go in regulating and controlling that information. The challenge here was to a law passed by Congress, the Communications Decency Act, which made it illegal to post any material or make any communication that was "indecent." The law did not clearly define what was "indecent," putting the burden on the person posting the materials or communication to risk that someone somewhere in the United States would be offended and file a criminal complaint against them.

The Supreme Court observed that at any given time "tens of thousands of users are engaging in conversations on a huge range of subjects." It stated that it was "no exaggeration to conclude that the content on the Internet is as diverse as human thought." But the Communications Decency Act, regardless of its good intentions, would scare people away from discussing or studying important subjects because of the risk of offending someone and then going to prison as a convicted felon. The Supreme Court noted:

> Under the CDA, a parent allowing her 17 year old to use the family computer to obtain information on the Internet that she, in her parental judgment, deems appropriate could face a lengthy prison term. See 47 U. S. C. A. §223(a)(2) (Supp. 1997). Similarly, a parent who sent his 17-year-old college freshman information on birth control via e-mail could be incarcerated even though neither he, his child, nor anyone in their home community, found the material "indecent" or "patently offensive," if the college town's community thought otherwise.

The Supreme Court found this vagueness in the CDA to be an illegal threat to free expression. The Court concluded:

> The dramatic expansion of this new marketplace of ideas contradicts the factual basis of this contention. The record demonstrates that the growth of the Internet has been and continues to be phenomenal. As a matter of constitutional tradition, in the absence of evidence to the contrary, we presume that governmental regulation of the content of speech is more likely to interfere with the free exchange of ideas than to encourage it. The interest in encouraging freedom of expression in a democratic society outweighs any theoretical but unproven benefit of censorship

The Supreme Court saw how the Internet offered great benefits in the exchange of knowledge and ideas, fundamental values for the United States. Its decision supported the expansion of that great exchange and limited the scope of efforts by government to regulate that at the expense of free speech.

But this court opinion is not the last word on this issue nor does it address the problem of the reliability of information online or the information crisis facing users of that great source of information.

WHY THE INTERNET IS THE WAY IT IS FOR SHARING INFORMATION

The Internet developed from a project of the Defense Advanced Research Projects Agency (DARPA). This project built a system for communicating among research scientists at key universities. DARPA is an agency of the United States Department of Defense responsible for some of the most cutting-edge research for national defense. The DARPA scientists knew and relied on each other's work in conducting their research. They did not build in security and safety features at first because they trusted each other and did not see the need.

A small exclusive group of scientists no longer controls the information on the Internet. That trusting relationship no longer protects its users. Any individual who wants to can post information on the Internet, from brilliant scholars to brilliant criminals to people who just do not know what they are talking about. A person's skills for assessing online information must both lead to good information and avoid what is dangerous and deceitful. A person's reputation, job, finances, health, and even their life and the lives of others, may depend on knowing what is true and what is false on the Internet.

THE PRICE OF FREEDOM AND WHAT IS AT STAKE

The right of speech free of government regulation comes with at least a moral and ethical responsibility to use that right properly. That responsibility includes posting speech that is as correct, accurate, and truthful as a person can make it, especially in the online world where it might be seen and used by anyone, from the very young to the very old.

Not all people act responsibly in their speech to assure truth and accuracy, nor do they know when *not* to accept irresponsible speech at face value. The truth can set people free, but only if it really is the truth. And the stakes can be very high and cover many aspects of people's lives where the truth is concerned. Consider, for example, information about children's health available from the Internet. Should someone trust the Internet for medical information about their child or little brother or sister?

In a 2009 study on Googling and children's health, Doctors Paul Scullard, Claire Peacock, and Patrick Davies decided to check this out in a systematic manner rather than simply relying on people's opinions.[2] They knew that 70 percent of households in their home country of the United Kingdom had Internet access. They knew that the Internet was a popular source of health information for parents, sometimes used even before the parents talked with a doctor or nurse. Earlier studies indicated that information on children's fevers, coughs, and tonsils could be very unreliable, as with information on adult health problems. To study this, they decided to act like parents using Google. Google was the most popular search engine, with parents using it to seek medical services for their children and even some doctors using it to access academic information.

To focus on the seriousness of the reliability issue, they chose five topics to search via related keywords. These included what to do when an infant throws up green vomit ("green vomit"), should infants sleep on their stomachs or on their backs ("baby sleeping position"), and is there a connection between the measles-mumps-rubella infant vaccinations and autism ("MMR autism"). While "green vomit" is usually not dangerous but may be worth a checkup by the doctor, it can scare a parent. On the other hand, not getting the MMR vaccination for a baby due to autism fears is potentially fatal to the infant.

The doctors looked at the first 100 Web sites returned on the Google search (limited to Web sites in Great Britain) and put the sites in various categories such as government, educational, news, commercial, and "sponsored," meaning someone paid for the link to be displayed. The medical advice was rated as "correct," "incorrect," or as not answering the questions. The results showed that of the information found, overall

- 39 percent gave correct information
- 11 percent gave incorrect information and
- 49 percent did not answer the questions

This is worrisome, but on some specific, serious issues the information provided was scary.

On the measles-mumps-rubella vaccine versus autism issue, 23 percent gave incorrect information versus 44 percent giving correct information. Which means that of the sites that actually offered an answer, one out of three gave bad information on a very serious, possibly life-threatening medical issue for children.

Even worse, on the issue of should an HIV-infected mother breast-feed her infant, 33 percent of sites gave incorrect information as opposed to only 35 percent giving correct advice. An HIV-infected mother should *never* breast-feed her infant, but of the Web sites answering this question only one out of two—about half—gave this correct information. Someone searching online for medical advice on this life-threatening issue had a 50-50 chance of getting the *wrong* information, with terrible, possibly fatal consequences for the baby. Scullard, Peacock, and Davies found both good and bad information on the Internet regarding sensitive health issues for children. Patterns emerged that offered some guidance as to where to look. They were able to offer these Reliability Rankings for UK medical information sites:

- Government Web sites were the best at giving correct information and should be "the first port of call for parents."
- Educational institutions, companies, special interest groups, and individual's Web sites were next, with about 80 percent correct information; even though concerns with individual motivations were noted, meaning there is still a risk with these sites, there was still good information.

- News sites and "sponsored" sites were the worst at providing correct information, with possible conflicts of interest in the sites' efforts to sell a product or promote controversy.

The doctors noted the limits to their study and possible biases in their selection of Web sites, although they felt theirs was a practical approach as to how people search for medical information on the Internet for their children. These British doctors underscored the essential need for education and understanding of medical issues by patients and parents.

Given the popularity and ease of the Internet for getting medical information, patients and parents need to be guided to good, reliable Web sites. This can better assure they get the best information possible and are steered clear of potentially bad and dangerous advice online.

Knowing how to properly act in the new online information world is not a simple thing. Most people do not have experience in saying what is right and proper online or knowing what responsibility someone has when they work online or with online technologies. This is *even true for the experts who design and build online systems*. This was enough of a concern that the National Science Foundation of the U.S. government funded Dr. Melissa Dark, Purdue University, and Dr. Linda Morales, University of Texas–Dallas, to look at these issues in new ways that would encourage reasoned, ethical ways of assuring trustworthy information in new systems. This responsibility would rest with those engineers and scientists designing new information systems. That would then help the people using those systems to know the risks they faced and ways to handle them. This is a warning not to rely on others for deciding reliability. For many people, new information technologies are risky because people do not know exactly how to respond to new, unexpected situations.

Dark, Morales, and their collaborators observed that safety with computing is much more than a technical issue that has a technical solution. Rather, it includes the intelligent and knowing involvement of people in assessing and avoiding risky conduct. This is as true

ONE CYBER WARRIOR IN THE RELIABILITY WARS

Dr. Deborah Frincke is a leading defender of assurance and trust in information and is the Deputy Director of Research for the U.S. Department of Defense (DOD) of the U.S. government. As chief scientist for cybersecurity research at the Pacific Northwest National Laboratory (PNNL) she led its internal research investment in cybersecurity, the Information and Infrastructure Integrity Initiative.

One theme of Dr. Frincke's work is that individuals using their reason and experience are more fundamental to, and probably more effective in, addressing cybersecurity and safety issues than simple technical solutions. She notes that despite the focus on outside "hackers" (though a serious threat), insiders remain some of the greatest dangers to cybersecurity as they are *already inside* the technical protections and firewalls. Dr. Frincke and her colleagues argue that applying traditional wisdom and caution, such as simply being skeptical about any assertion without support, is a good use of information resources whether in print or online.

whether a person is assessing the validity of information from an online source or the danger that online source will plant a drive-by malware virus on their computer.

Their work fosters a more mature understanding of how people build, use, and act with online information tools.

THE POWER OF THE NEWEST INFORMATION TOOL

This big tool, the Internet, composed of services such as the World Wide Web, e-mail, chat, Skype, and many others, is really like a huge toolbox that contains a collection of tools, attachments, and add-ons for doing many different things.

The right tool in the toolbox, sometimes combined with other tools, can make the lessons, information and wisdom of classrooms, friends, discussions, town halls, TV, and talk radio available almost anywhere at any time. It puts all that under the control of the people using them. With that control, people can read, watch, or listen, and even take that information and transform it into things like the new analysis of a term paper, a new music mashup of songs, or the creation of ideas and expression no one has thought of yet.

The vast virtual world library of computers called the Internet uses tools such as powerful searchable databases to compute information and then render it in ways people can use it. These tools also allow the analysis, manipulation, and use of those information files in new and different ways.

But it is still important to remember the old lesson of "garbage in, garbage out." If a person is going to rely on someone else's information for their new work or creations, they must verify that it is good information they will be using and not someone else's "garbage."

The online world is still evolving, becoming more powerful yet more and more a regular part of daily life. "Cloud computing," for example, expressly uses the power of all the available computers on the Internet in all its forms for the benefit of each person using it. Cloud computing shares information, storage, media, software, and computing power as requested by a user, similar to utility services like water or power. The MasterBase Glossary of Technology Terms describes cloud computing as "a technology used to access services offered on the Internet cloud. Everything an information system has to offer is provided as a service, so users can access these services available on the 'Internet cloud' without having any previous know-how (or at least not as an expert) on managing the resources involved."[3] In other words, it turns an Internet device, whether a computer, tablet, or smartphone, into a connection to powerful computers and services all over the Internet and all over the world all the time.

Working in the "cloud" moves beyond just storing information in the Internet world library to treating everything as a potential

Attendees walk by a sign for the iCloud, a storage device that utilizes cloud computing, during the 2011 Apple World Wide Developers Conference at the Moscone Center in San Francisco, California. (*Justin Sullivan/Getty Images*)

resource to use. The "cloud" of interconnected Internet computers will offer more and more of these tools to do all the information retrieval, game playing, and computing out in the cloud. All a person will need is a tool to send the request into the cloud and show the result sent back. That tool will be like a Web browser, seamlessly handling everything. It gives every person the possibility of a supercomputer they can hold in their hands.

The Internet cloud may offer huge advances in computing power as the average person may be able to use a remote supercomputer from any device.

The trade-off is that the user will have to use that immense power responsibly, even when given that power with little or no training in how to use it. There is still no technical substitute for using the ability to reason each person possesses to discern the truth and act

DEFINING THE CLOUD

The National Institute for Standards and Technology (NIST), the first federal physical sciences laboratory, is charged with developing technology, measurements, and standards for science, engineering, and industry. Though noting that the very idea of cloud computing continues to change, NIST has developed its definition of cloud computing as a way to organize how people can talk about it. NIST states:

Definition of Cloud Computing:
Cloud computing is a model for enabling ubiquitous, convenient, on-demand network access to a shared pool of configurable computing resources (e.g., networks, servers, storage, applications, and services) that can be rapidly provisioned and released with minimal management effort or service provider interaction. This cloud model promotes availability and is composed of five essential characteristics, three service models, and four deployment models.[4]

The cloud's **essential characteristics** are that services are always available on-demand with broad network access, a pooling of resources to get work done while expanding as needed, and the ability to measure and monitor the services provided. The three **service models** are that the software, the platforms on which it runs, and the whole infrastructure of storage and networks are all available as services a customer can access. And the **deployment models** let clouds be set up for individual organizations, communities, the general public, and as hybrid combinations of them. This is only a start in the effort to understand what the cloud is and how it can help people work better on and off the Internet.

responsibly. No machine can do that. But reason is not as easy to use as Google. Or Facebook. A person has to sit and think. Perhaps even think for a while, even with everyone else wanting an immediate response. When would a person decide to take that extra effort to critically think about, say, information they found on the Internet instead of just taking it at face value? What is the risk?

HOW BAD IT CAN BE: INTERNET RUMORS AND SNOPES.COM

The dangers of bad things on the Internet are exemplified by the rumors it hosts and spreads faster than cafeteria gossip. Internet rumors fly so fast and far that people now devote Web sites to tracking and discussing them and, when possible, separating the truth from the fantasy. David and Barbara Mikkelson have made that truth-tracking a mission run out of their home. Their Web site is Snopes.com, the leader in the Internet rumor-tracking business. It is named for a disturbing family detailed in William Faulkner's novels.

The Mikkelsons began, in 1995, examining urban legends and commenting on them over the UseNet news system of the early Internet. Their work on urban legends, modern folklore, and e-rumors expanded into their advertising-supported Web site, one of the most popular and reliable on the Internet. Their work has been the subject of articles in the *New York Times*, the *Wall Street Journal*, and the *Washington Post*, and on National Public Radio. In 2009, *Readers Digest* ran a story on them, "Rumor Detectives: True Story or Online Hoax?"

Snopes.com has thousands of articles and discussions of rumors and stories throughout the Internet. Their articles contain their research and evaluation of those stories, many of which have been around for years and are recycled with new features added. One example is the 1990s rumor that President Bill Clinton, to save money, had ordered half the cattle guards in Colorado fired, not realizing a cattle guard is just a rail bridge cars can pass over but cattle will not. That rumor has returned, but this time with President Barack Obama as the culprit. A good rumor, even if false, just never seems to end.

Other online rumors Snopes.com has tracked down are that people will get cash or computers from Microsoft for sending on a

THE IMPACT OF SOCIAL NETWORKING

Does the super-connected Internet world overwhelm people and distract them from thoughtful living? Might the cloud lead to clouded thinking? Or even the dull avoidance of considered thought about things? One writer even posed the question "Is Google Making Us Stupid?"[5] Maybe the Internet is not affecting people that severely, but it may be changing behavior for some people.

Social media like Facebook are part of that. Keith Hampton, Lauren Sessions Goulet, Lee Rainie, and Kristen Purcell studied whether or not being active on social networking sites would make people less social and less involved with others in the "real" world. This was an effort by the Pew Research Center's Internet and American Life Project to see how social media might impact "trust, tolerance, social support, and community and political engagement."[6]

The researchers surveyed 2,255 adults ages 18 and over, where Facebook was the predominant social networking site used by

chain e-mail (FALSE), that a bill is pending in Congress to require gun owners to declare their firearms on their tax returns (FALSE), and that big horn sheep can climb the sheer walls of the Buffalo Bill Dam in Wyoming (often with real photos but of Italian goats climbing the sheer wall of an Italian dam; so mostly FALSE). On the other hand, Snopes.com found as true such stories as identity thieves pretending to call people about jury duty to get personal information. Their research and fact checking cuts both ways.

In 2010, David Mikkelson was interviewed by the *New York Times* about the astounding popularity of rumors. Mikkelson suggested rumors fly because people try to help others, not realizing the falsity or the rumor, or they are trying to prove their own

92 percent of respondents, followed by MySpace at 29 percent, LinkedIn at 18 percent, and Twitter at 13 percent. They found that, in comparison to the average American, Facebook users were more socially engaged:

- Facebook users were more trusting than others.
- Facebook users had more close relationships.
- Facebook users received more social support than others.
- Facebook users were more politically active than others.
- Facebook let people reopen old relationships with people they had not spoken with in some time.

They found no evidence that social network users were more likely to lock themselves away from the wider world of opinions by only associating with people who only thought the way they did. In fact, they found that users of MySpace were more likely to be open to considering multiple and opposing points of view than the average person. This seems to show that social networking is having a positive impact on how people work together.

misperceptions about things, especially where prejudice outweighs reason. To demonstrate how rumors get started Snopes.com made up a fake story about how a nursery rhyme was a secret way for pirates to recruit sailors in taverns and, sure enough, it ended up being recited as fact. Most disturbing was one of the last questions asked Mikkelson:

David Pogue: You would think that with the instant communications of Internet, that all this misinformation and urban legend stuff—that people would catch on that it's not true.

David Mikkelson: The flaw in that theory is that for a good many people, it's not important whether things are true or not. It reflects what people want to believe. It reflects a worldview. It's their way of passing along things that concern them. Things they're afraid of.[7]

With success comes, of course, rumors. The Mikkelsons were attacked in a chain e-mail for being pro-Democrat liberals and "hiding" after a story they posted on a politically oriented insurance agent's sign. The chain e-mail alleged that the Mikkelsons were politically biased, factually inaccurate, and had not attempted to contact people involved in the story.

FactCheck.org, an online political rumor-hunter of the Annenberg Public Policy Center of the University of Pennsylvania, checked it out and found the allegations false. Yet another urban attack myth. Some people just do not like the truth, an important lesson to always remember.

In an interview with National Public Radio,[8] David Mikkelson noted, "What we've learned over time is there's pretty much nothing that you can immediately dismiss as too absurd to be true."

People who use the Internet and components like the World Wide Web need the tools to get the information files and the skill to use them reliably and safely. That skill means following basic rules for judging the "quality" of information, sometimes referred to as the reliability of the information. Every person using the Internet should learn those rules and use them. Otherwise, they leave the door open to embarrassment or injury, to themselves or to others.

Researching
Information Online

Jennifer sat rocking in her chair, holding her baby. Things were not going well. Her boyfriend, the baby's father, had dropped her when he learned she was pregnant. He wasn't providing her any support at all to help with their child, although, thank God, her family was there for her. And his last "gift" to her was an STD he had never told her about, one for which there was no cure. But her baby, John, was healthy and she was determined he would grow up healthy and happy and able to survive without her.

Jennifer was doing home study while John was young. She began using her online search skills to see what was best for her baby, in addition to doing her homework. A lot of Web sites talked about the importance of breast-feeding a baby to keep it healthy. Jennifer was concerned about her illness and whether breast-feeding might hurt her baby. When she asked those specific questions, the Web sites she first found said that there was no danger and that it greatly improves a child's chances of a healthy life. So Jennifer began breast-feeding baby John, neglecting to ask her doctor about it before she started.

When she took baby John in for his checkup several months later, the nurse asked her what kind of formula she was feeding him. Jennifer told the nurse that she had been breast-feeding; the nurse looked startled, asked to be excused, and left the room. A few minutes later she returned with the pediatrician, who also had a concerned look on her face. Jennifer repeated what she had said to the doctor, who first told her that she needed to stop breast-feeding him and start using baby formula for John. The nurse came back and said they had to do a blood test for baby John but that there was nothing to worry about at that point. Otherwise, baby John was doing fine.

The doctor's office called back the next week and asked Jennifer to come back in with baby John. When she arrived Jennifer was taken to a room with the doctor, the nurse, and a lady from the public health department. Jennifer felt the dread in her heart before the doctor began speaking. As if from far away, the doctor told her that John, too, was now infected with her illness. The nurse and the public health lady would go over with her what she would need to do to keep John well for as long as possible.

When she finished, Jennifer started to cry and said that she had tried to do her best and that the Internet sites she found said it was okay to breast-feed John even with her illness.

The doctor, her lips now pressed together in a tight, bitter line, said, "They were wrong. Very, very wrong. I'm so sorry."

With the Internet it is now possible to quickly conduct significant background research on a topic or project that in the past only large corporations, governments, or universities could afford to do.

A core question is where and with what tool to start that research. The next is what the proper use of that tool is, and what the danger from its misuse is. Internet research tools come in several forms. Generally all of these tools let a user enter keywords that have a particular relevance and importance to what a person wishes to know. The search tool then tries to find the most appropriate responses to these keywords within its collection of information.

The tools with the biggest scope on the Internet are search engines, like Google, Yahoo, and Bing. These search engines scour the Internet for every Web page they can find. They then analyze each of these Web pages, index the words on it, and examine the words within it and the links to and from other sites that connect to it. Using these and other techniques, search engines try and provide the most relevant response to a particular search.

Other tools are more focused, such as Web sites that provide access to collections of information on particular topics in particular ways and are supported by organizations that assure reliability to varying degrees. Some resources are like Wikipedia, which is an online searchable encyclopedia supported by public participation that stores information and discussions on individual topics; in some areas it is very reliable and in others there have been issues with inaccurate information. Other Web sites focus on very specific kinds of knowledge, such as legal, health, or sports information that can also be searched by entering keyword terms but are supported in a variety of ways.

With all of these a person using the Internet research tool must be careful to assure the reliability of the information found, as there are so few controls and restrictions on information that is placed on the Internet.

ABOUT WIKIPEDIA

A good example to study is Wikipedia, loved by students and disliked by teachers and judges. That conflict precisely illustrates what is at stake with the use of any online tool in the pursuit of truth. Wikipedia is a very popular tool, though perhaps not the best tool for research for all information. But it has never claimed to be. Wikipedia primarily serves to collect information for which it encourages people to post reliably. It tries to offer users substantial information overviews and sources under a series of carefully crafted guidelines but puts the burden of verifying that information on the Wikipedia users themselves.

WHEN OPINION BECOMES "TRUTH" IN WIKIPEDIA

Wikipedia depends on its community of supporters to assure the reliability of its information. But its open, democratic nature offers opportunities for highly passionate people to post things that may be much more opinion than fact.

For example, when Kathleen Sibelius, the United States Secretary of Health and Human Services, was governor of Kansas, she was known as a supporter for the right to keep and bear arms. This was reflected on a Wikipedia page about her, but then someone decided to change "is" to "is not" and an entirely different message was sent. How or why would this happen? And could it impact something as important as the election of a political leader?

The political Web site Governing.com asserts that Wikipedia's ability to be super current on developments lets political operatives manipulate and "spin" facts about political leaders, especially close to elections.[1] Wikipedia's volunteers police such actions and other acts of vandalism, as it was designed, but there is still a window where lies can overcome truth.

Wikipedia is a much used and much criticized online data compilation. As an "open source" system it is open to editing by everyone in the world. It relies on a huge army of volunteers to constantly check its information for accuracy and reliability. But, as a result, there are people who have tried to "spoof" (cheat) and place fake or inaccurate information in Wikipedia. Despite this, in some areas, Wikipedia is as reliable as traditional sources in providing information. The question for every user is how they can possibly know which is which.

It is not only teachers who dislike Wikipedia and forbid students from using it for authority in class papers.

Jimmy Wales, founder of Wikipedia and Wikimedia, speaks during a conference at Harvard University. (*AP Photo/Lisa Poole*)

The Philippines Court of Appeals hammered a government lawyer for relying on Wikipedia for crucial expert evidence in a trial. In
doing so, that court noted that Wikipedia itself cautions readers and
users as to the reliability of its open source model.

In that case the prosecutor for the Office of the Solicitor General
(OSG) of the Philippines was faced with a psychiatric expert witness
testifying on behalf of his opponent that the parties suffered from
psychological incapacity. He did not do the expected and produce
his own psychiatric witness. Rather, to contradict the psychiatrist he
introduced evidence taken from Wikipedia regarding mental health
issues.[2]

The Court of Appeals said that using such information as evidence in the judicial proceeding was "incredible . . . if not a haphaz-
ard attempt, on the part of the [OSG] to impeach an expert witness,
with, as pointed out by [the ex-wife], unreliable information. This is
certainly unacceptable evidence, nothing short of a mere allegation
totally unsupported by authority."

It was not a good day in court, but it provides a good lesson
for Internet users.[3] Wikipedia can be a valuable pointer to begin
research, but a person should not rely on it as the final word.

Might Wikipedia Still Be a Useful Tool?

Wikipedia describes itself as a collaborative information tool
supported by volunteers who decide what should be included.
Wikipedia acknowledges its critics, who claim it is more of a
popularity contest on knowledge rather than a reference that
relies on competent experts. Wikipedia notes that the expertise
or qualifications of contributors are not usually considered, as its
goal is to "cover existing knowledge which is verifiable from other
sources."[8]

Wikipedia sets out standards for the validation of information it
offers, such as encouraging the use of citations to supporting references. Its volunteers add comments in support and point out missing
supporting references and questionable claims. Wikipedia expressly
states that newer discussions are particularly susceptible to bad and

BE CAREFUL WITH WIKIPEDIA

In one federal criminal prosecution the defendant, convicted by a jury of extortion, lying to federal investigators, and retaliating against a witness, asked the trial judge for a new trial. Among other reasons, she said that her lawyer rendered "ineffective assistance of counsel" in that he did not properly defend her in her criminal trial. In denying that request, the trial judge wrote:

> The court notes here that defense counsel appears to have cobbled much of his statement of the law governing ineffective assistance of counsel claims by cutting and pasting, without citation, from the Wikipedia Web site. *Compare* Supplemental to Motion for New Trial (DN 199) at 18–19 *with* http://en.wikipedia.org/wiki/Strickland_v._Washington (last visited Feb. 9, 2011). . . . the court reminds counsel that Wikipedia is not an acceptable source of legal authority in the United States District Courts.[4]

The defendant denied the judge's assertions and asked the judge to remove himself from the case for this investigation of the defendant's legal work[5]; the judge declined to do so[6] and sentenced the defendant to seven years and three months in prison.[7]

inaccurate information and even vandalism, where some people *intentionally* post false information to mislead, defame, or hurt others. Wikipedia warns users to validate and verify what they find on its site. Wikipedia is, in effect, a potentially good *pointer* to information. But it should never be the end of the search for information on something really important. Like a grade. Or a court case. Or a health and medical decision. Or for whom to vote.

Wikipedia freely admits: "Wikipedia can be a great tool for learning and researching information. However, as with all sources, not everything in Wikipedia is accurate, comprehensive, or unbiased. Many of the general rules of thumb for conducting research apply to Wikipedia, including:

- Always be wary of any one single source (in any medium—Web, print, television or radio), or of multiple works that derive from a single source.
- Where articles have references to external sources (whether online or not) read the references and check whether they really do support what the article says.
- In most academic institutions, Wikipedia, along with most encyclopedias, is unacceptable as a major source for a research paper. Other encyclopedias, such as *Encyclopædia Britannica*, have notable authors working for them and may be cited as a secondary source in most cases. For example, Cornell University has a guide on how to cite encyclopedias."[9]

Just as teachers require footnotes and citations to research cited in student work, Wikipedia prefers entries to be footnoted with references to other sources to support what is being said. These footnoted comments may also have hyperlinks to other Wikipedia references to help a reader check on what is being said from within the information collection. These are ways of verifying the reliability of what is claimed, increasingly important in the online world.

It seems odd to cite Wikipedia for why a person should not cite Wikipedia. But it is, in fact, a good example of an online source that is willing to say up front that it is not a completely reliable source and that anyone using it should do a lot more checking. Unfortunately, few online sources do this for the people who use them.

As Wikipedia states:

This page in a nutshell: You should not use Wikipedia by itself for primary research (unless you are writing a paper about Wikipedia).[10]

Wikipedia may drive teachers crazy when students cite it, but note how Wikipedia is willing to say what its critics say about it and its flaws. An important sign of intellectual integrity is the willingness to note and address criticism, not hide from it.

Far too many people want to hide from criticism and critique. But though it can be painful or embarrassing, the ability to consider and learn from good criticism (and reject criticism without a basis) lets people learn and progress to better and better work.

Wikipedia warns of the risks from its open source, social network model of globally collecting information from anyone willing to help. Yet at the same time it is a place to start researching a topic, if a person has no idea where else to start. Its collaborative model, though with potential problems, has helped many people learn new things with a level of reliability to continue their search for knowledge.

This phenomena as to reliability and security has caught the interest of academics for use in other areas, particularly that of cybersecurity. The possibilities of such social networks for enhancing cybersecurity are significant, if realized. In other words, this model holds promise to help people in many other online areas, but only if people know how to use it properly and carefully.

A SPECIAL TOPICS WEB SITE: THE INTERNET ENCYCLOPEDIA OF PHILOSOPHY

One contrast to Wikipedia is the Internet Encyclopedia of Philosophy. Like Wikipedia, the Internet Encyclopedia of Philosophy is a volunteer project. But in contrast to Wikipedia, the Internet Encyclopedia of Philosophy is a much more controlled system.

This Web site outlines, among other philosophers, the life and works of Sir Francis Bacon and his efforts to change the way people examine information and knowledge. Its volunteer staff members are all highly qualified in their areas of study, holding doctorate degrees, and are teachers in various colleges. The Internet Encyclopedia of Philosophy uses a vetting process like print journals and books, requiring authors to be specialists in the subjects on which they write.

(continues on page 44)

WHAT WIKIPEDIA SAYS ABOUT WIKIPEDIA AND HOW TRUSTWORTHY IT IS

Wikipedia and the people who support it have the integrity to describe what it does, how it works, and how reliable its information is. Wikipedia relies on the integrity of the people making contributions and on key rules to help users of Wikipedia verify that they may rely on the information posted. Wikipedia notes:

> Wikipedia is a free, Web-based, collaborative, multilingual encyclopedia project supported by the non-profit Wikimedia Foundation. Its 18 million articles (over 3.5 million in English) have been written collaboratively by volunteers around the world, and almost all of its articles can be edited by anyone with access to the site. Wikipedia was launched in 2001 by Jimmy Wales and Larry Sanger and has become the largest and most popular general reference work on the Internet, ranking around seventh among all Web sites on Alexa and having 365 million readers. . . .
>
> Although the policies of Wikipedia strongly espouse verifiability and a neutral point of view, critics of Wikipedia accuse it of systemic bias and inconsistencies (including undue weight given to popular culture), and allege that it favors consensus over credentials in its editorial processes. Its reliability and accuracy are also targeted.[11] Other criticisms center on its susceptibility to vandalism and the addition of spurious or unverified information, though scholarly work suggests that vandalism is generally short-lived, and an investigation in *Nature* found that the science articles they compared came close to the level of accuracy of *Encyclopædia Britannica* and had a similar rate of "serious errors."
>
> Wikipedia's departure from the expert-driven style of the encyclopedia building mode and the large presence of unacademic

content have been noted several times. When *Time* magazine recognized "You" as its Person of the Year for 2006, acknowledging the accelerating success of online collaboration and interaction by millions of users around the world, it cited Wikipedia as one of several examples of Web 2.0 services, along with YouTube, MySpace, and Facebook. Some noted the importance of Wikipedia not only as an encyclopedic reference but also as a frequently updated news resource because of how quickly articles about recent events appear. Students have been assigned to write Wikipedia articles as an exercise in clearly and succinctly explaining difficult concepts to an uninitiated audience.[12]

So there are important concerns with Wikipedia and its reliability. But for a popular topic that many people participate in updating, it can be a starting place, as long as a person does not stop there. Which for too many people, it is too easy to do.

And there is the problem of less popular topics being dominated by a small number of people who might not be so careful about what they post or who do not have the time to correct blatantly incorrect information. As noted before, Wikipedia has had problems with vandals trying to skew its information to support someone's personal agenda.

At least one test case involved someone intentionally placing incorrect information on Wikipedia to see if people would catch it. Not only was it not caught quickly, but a number of national print publications used the incorrect information from Wikipedia as authority (uncredited) in their publications. Very scary!

Another disturbing trend has developed. Wikipedia relies on many people participating, contributing, editing, and fact checking what others say in its articles. There has been a decrease in people participating in those roles. With fewer writers, editors, and fact-checkers, will Wikipedia continue to be as rich a source of information as it is?

(continued from page 41)

Their submissions are then "peer-reviewed" by other specialists in the area who may accept the article, reject it, or return it with recommendations for revisions and changes. This is typical of the academic review process that helps assure the reliability of the submission and its worth for inclusion in the Internet Encyclopedia of Philosophy. It notes that if there are no submissions for a particular subject then the encyclopedia will use public domain materials as temporary material in those areas.

The Internet Encyclopedia of Philosophy uses other "indicators of reliability" of Internet information that offer assurance that it is a reliable resource.

One important indicator of reliability is that the Internet Encyclopedia of Philosophy, http://www.iep.utm.edu, is hosted by a recognized, accredited university, the University of Tennessee at Martin (the "utm.edu" in the Web address). The general editors are faculty at the University of Tennessee, philosophy professor James Fieser, and California State University at Sacramento philosophy professor Bradley Dowden. Universities and their faculty have high standards for the quality and ethics of the work they produce and support, so this assures that the work in the encyclopedia is good and reliable.

Further investigation supports the credibility of the Internet Encyclopedia of Philosophy. Other sources reference its material, as can be seen from a simple Google search. Indeed, one article critical of Wikipedia for its openness to amateur writers and abusive posters holds up the Internet Encyclopedia of Philosophy with its high standards as the model for excellent, quality online publishing.[13]

It is always important to know how useful and reliable a resource is and to use it accordingly.

Good Computing Leads to Good Information

Victoria was worried about her weight and her figure. "How big a teenage cliché is that?" she thought.

She and her fellow classmates had all been through the tedious class presentations on proper health practices by young adults on, among other things, anorexia and bulimia. The presentations in class had been very clear about long-term health dangers of self-starvation and forced vomiting, especially the stomach acids eroding the teeth. Victoria flashed her teeth in the mirror, all clean and white and straight. But several other girls with nice trim and slim figures privately told her that anorexia and bulimia worked for them, even the binge eating and binge vomiting that seemed so gross. They said the teachers were just overreacting and that there was a lot of good information on the Internet explaining the benefits of being "pro–Ana."

Sure enough, Victoria found a lot of information on the Internet about the benefits of anorexia and bulimia in keeping a good figure. But who were the people providing it?

As Victoria read through the pages of their testimonials and even through quizzes about "are you ready to be a pro–Ana?" she felt more and more uneasy. Their language, their stridency, their tone all began to remind her of the people she knew who didn't really think about what they were saying. "Geez, is this some kind of cult?" she wondered. It was simply getting too weird as discussion boards on the sites turned into nasty, angry attacks back and forth.

Victoria sat back. "Well, that went nowhere. Except now I know this is a more dangerous issue than I'd thought. So I'm still stuck with more exercise and less soda. But that's better than stepping off into other people's fantasies of what I should be like and what I should do."

With the Internet as a great information tool comes increasing danger. Anyone can provide information over the Internet, including people who are spiteful. Some of these people try to hurt others even if they do not know them. There are also people who are simply uninformed or wrong about what they know. They do not really mean to harm anyone, but they will say things without checking the facts. If a person does not verify what is said, he or she may end up relying on bad information.

No one yet fully knows how the Internet is changing people's lives, although the Pew Research Center study of social networks indicates they are having a positive influence.

One thing is clear: The connectedness of the Internet brings together people and information that would never have come together before.

Growing up in the pre-Internet world, a person might have lived in a neighborhood with 50 or 60 neighbors. A person might have gone to religious services with a similar number of other people. That same person might have gone to school with several hundred other students and teachers, with a library of two or three thousand books. But on the Internet a person is virtually one step away from hundreds of millions of other people and billions of Web pages. Every one of them can connect and put out information with no guarantee of trustworthiness or responsibility.

Coming together is how people share new ideas and understanding. But it can also create risks that can only be overcome with the use of care and reason. Every Web page visit, every search, every tweet or squirt of text connects one computer to another, computing and transmitting information from one person to another.

Critical and intelligent computing helps avoid the dangers of the information crisis. Good computing is the foundation for good information.

GOOD COMPUTING AS COMMUNITY SERVICE

Several universities have taken up good computing in society as part of service learning and community engagement in their engineering and science programs. For example, Purdue University's Engineering Projects in Community Service (EPICS) project supports teams working on iPad applications (apps) and Google Android apps for assistive technology. Twenty universities collaborate in the national EPICS effort. The University of Louisville's Department of Computer Engineering and Computer Science weaves community engagement into coursework through hardware/software development and community teaching and service projects. One such project began with community presentations regarding computer security and safe computer use to avoid viruses, Trojan horses, spam, spyware, phishing, and online fraud attacks.

Good computing—the right way to use computing devices—is at the heart of working through the information crisis. As with the successful use of any tool, it requires that the person using the computing tool do so properly, competently, and wisely. All people need to start with the right way of computing to get the knowledge they need and avoid the problems they may otherwise encounter.

COMPETENT USE

The crux of the information crisis is that too many people trust what they read without verifying the information, as if the computer has a magical reliability. Supposedly Pierre Gallois caught the sense of this when he wrote:

> If you put tomfoolery into a computer, nothing comes out of it but tomfoolery. But this tomfoolery, having passed through a very expensive machine, is somehow ennobled and no-one dares criticize it.

But, then, who was Pierre Gallois? Although this is a popular quote about the trickiness of information reliability, it has been variously attributed to Pierre Gallois, the French military expert and general, and Pierre Gallois, the French scientist. Which is correct?[1] This is one example of how slippery verification can be.

Intelligent use of computing and the Internet is a combination of three types of skills:

- technical
- critical thinking
- social/legal

Technical Skills with the Internet

Technical skills are those related to effective searching, access, and transmittal of information. These functions are relatively easy due to the powerful tools now available, such as Google, but technical skills can help. Technical skills include search skills. The most popular searching systems are search engines that simply require entry of search terms and a click of a submission button. But search accuracy can be improved by better use of search techniques.

These include:

- *Choose the appropriate search system.* A particular search engine might be better at searching in a particular content area or type of information than others. Google seems to be the current leader for general searching, but LexisNexis might be better for legal research. Shopping search systems might be better focused on prices while engines designed around typical questions people have, like Yahoo! Answers, might be better for quick answers to common questions.

- *Choose the appropriate search terms.* It is really important to choose only those key words that are most relevant to the desired search, as those are the starting point from which the search engines begin their analysis. Too many or too broad a selection of search terms/key words can give results that do not answer the question or are so numerous that time is wasted wading through them.

- *Use special functions to direct the searching.* Several search engines offer special features to help improve the responsiveness of the search. In Google and Yahoo!, for example, these are called "Advanced Search" features. They permit a searcher to refine the search based on such features as requiring some terms, excluding others, limiting to certain time periods and Web sites and other factors that may improve the search results.[2]

Critical Thinking Skills

The information crisis is about trustworthiness. How can *anything* on the Internet be trusted? Thinking critically about information found on the Internet can avoid many problems.

The trust crisis is a huge issue. It ranges from information that tricks children and teenagers to identity theft and fraud to attacks against the United States.

There are many efforts to try and improve the trustworthiness of the Internet. But the first line of defense is the oldest: people should trust those they know can be trusted. If a source is unknown, a person should use *reason* and *resources* to see if it can be trusted. In other words, critically analyze everything. Once people master the tools for getting information, they must then judge its value. That converts the information to knowledge that can be used successfully and safely.

The major difference between the Internet and most real world libraries at school or in the community is this: the librarian, whether a trained professional or a parent, chooses books based on their assessment as to value and quality. But *everything* gets on the Internet.

People online become their own librarian. *They* become responsible for deciding what information is useful and reliable and what is garbage, or worse.

This can be tough as it is hard to know what one does not know. Especially with the rise of the Internet criminal class, ready and willing to tell people what to know and what to do so they can become their victims.

If a person's family and teachers (and sometimes friends) push them hard to think *critically* and judge things for, say, truthfulness, wisdom, and kindness, that person has a good start. He or she has a foundation for being able to tell if Internet information is good or bad. But if not and a person grows up told to listen and obey and not to question, then they must make the extra effort to learn how to judge the real value of what they find online.

For parents and teachers, guardians and leaders, this can be tough to accept. But there is no alternative. And this is not a new challenge.

Hundreds of years ago an English scholar, scientist, politician, and statesman, Sir Francis Bacon, and other scholars were unhappy with foolish and superstitious ideas being accepted as truth. Things like the ability to change lead into gold (alchemy) or "magicks." So they developed a method of testing the reliability of information that Bacon called "The New Tool." The New Tool was meant to challenge the "idols" of foolishness. That new tool is what is today called the scientific method of research and validation. It has led to, among other things, the new knowledge that led to the creation of the Internet.

English philosopher, essayist, and statesman Sir Francis Bacon's promotion of scientific inquiry contributed to the development of the scientific method. (*Stock Montage/Getty Images*)

Legal and Social Issues with Internet Information

The law and social rules of the Internet are still evolving. People lack experience with proper ways to act. That lack includes an understanding of the legal and social consequences of what people do online. A person on the Internet must be aware of some of these potential problems, even someone with good intentions.

For example, people have gossiped about others for a long time, but the impact was limited. Now gossip online reaches tens of thousands of people and can cause a great deal of damage to someone. It may be permanently recorded in an electronic writing somewhere. What once might have been lost or forgotten can become a slander lawsuit. All because some are not careful online about the truth of what they say and the harm caused from saying it.

THE COMPUTER AND ITS APPLICATIONS

The Internet information tool includes millions of computing machines, from laptops to smartphones and other devices, and various tools known as applications, or "apps," that retrieve, manage, and display and play the information.

Computing devices come in many different forms, from tablets to smartphones. They can connect through a variety of wireless and wired connections.

Once connected, other tools are needed to find, retrieve, render, and manage the information. They navigate the Internet as a ship navigates across the sea.

Each of these features has its purpose. One finds information and requests that a remote computer send that information to the user's device. The features may also help manage the information.

Some of these sub-tools include:

- a Web browser
- e-mail
- IM/telephony/Twitter
- add-ons for special features, such as media players, Acrobat, Flash, and so on

THE NEW TOOL
AND THE SCIENTIFIC METHOD

Critical thinking might be considered a tool to come closer to the truth. What is called the "scientific method" is a process of making judgments as to truth. Sir Francis Bacon challenged his peers, who believed they could accept only knowledge from the scholars of the past. He set out his new ideas about knowledge in his book *Novum Organum*, translated variously as "New Tool," "New Instrument," or "New Logic."

His "New Tool" required a person to observe the world, apply the intellect to those observations, and then test any conclusions to see if they held up.

Sir Francis wrote what might be called one of the earliest "science fiction" novels, *New Atlantis*, wherein people, using their reason, experimented and studied the world in order to produce new, useful inventions. This book proposed that a research institution was needed, much like the modern research universities of today.

Though a great scholar and scientist, Sir Francis became the Lord Chancellor of England, one of the most powerful men in the nation, only to be disgraced and removed for bribery. His life was one of rise and fall. He admitted his error and accepted his punishment and continued his work to advance knowledge and learning for the betterment of all people.

More on Sir Francis Bacon is available at the Internet Encyclopedia of Philosophy at http://www.iep.utm.edu/bacon. Before reading, consider how Sir Francis might expect the information about him to be judged. Consider how to critically analyze that portrayal and his life.

These tools have become easy to use. With more use, people learn about the more powerful features that let them do more. With practice, reading, and research online, or tips from friends, people can master them.

Web Browsers

The competition for the best browser is ongoing and intense. The contest is generally split between computers using Windows and those from Apple. But competition is coming from new systems, especially handheld devices that use operating systems like Linux and Android. Some of those Web browsers are:

For Windows
Explorer
Firefox
Apple Safari
Opera
Chrome

For Apple
Apple Safari
Opera
Firefox
Chrome

For Linux
Firefox
Chrome
Opera

Windows Explorer is the most widely used browser, with Firefox and Chrome, respectively, second and third most used.[3]

Web browsers store Web site addresses for later use, including in folders for grouping similar Web sites. Additional features offer easier and safer use, as, unfortunately, more Web sites are used to push unwanted advertising, or, sometimes, dangerous malware, on to unsuspecting visitors.

But the computer and Web browsers are only starting spots for getting information. As the amount of information online has grown, it has become more difficult to know where to find what. To overcome this problem, search engines can help guide the search for information.

Microsoft Corp.'s Windows Internet Explorer is displayed next to the Mozilla Corp.'s Firefox Web browser on a computer screen. Internet Explorer and Firefox are two of the most-used Web browsers. (*Bloomberg via Getty Images*)

THE TECHNOLOGY OF THE TOOL: SEARCHING

Mastering this new world requires using information retrieval tools to their best. These tools may help weigh the relevance, reliability, and completeness of what a person has found online.

Relevance means that the information a person has found is what they want. Reliability means the person can use the information with some degree of certainty. Completeness means they've found all the information they need on a subject and something important was not left out.

The Internet is so huge that it is difficult, if not impossible, for humans to review it all for relevance. Reliability and completeness are even more difficult. Determining whether or not one can rely on the information and that it is complete is sometimes a decision only an expert can make. The new search tools can help with this task.

WEB BROWSER FEATURES AND SEARCH POWER TOOLS

The Web browser tools for gathering information from Web sites have evolved over the last 20 years. Newer features and add-ons for the ever-expanding new multimedia are offered over the Internet. Buttons and tabs for switching among different Web pages help navigation. Menus and toolbars provide more choices and services with browsers similar to word processing programs like Word. Information retrieved can be saved and printed, or selected, copied, and pasted elsewhere. The appearance of a Web page can be changed so that the size of the text can be increased or other character sets, like Chinese, can be displayed. And privacy settings can be used to protect privacy from people trying to track what Web pages an individual visits. Search capabilities have evolved as well.

The most popular general search services, some of which share the same search engines, are:

- Google—http://www.google.com
- Yahoo!—http://search.yahoo.com (uses the Bing engine)
- Bing—http://www.bing.com
- AOL—http://search.aol.com (uses the Google engine)
- Ask—http://www.ask.com
- Exalead—http://www.exalead.com/search

Google

Google, the leading search engine, tries to assure quality, relevance, and reliability through the online equivalent of voting, sort of like *American Idol* or a trial jury. Among other test and evaluation procedures it uses, Google scans a Web page and then scans and reviews the Internet to see how many other Web pages link to that Web page. Google treats each link like a vote of confidence, so the more links to a particular Web page the higher Google ranks it as being more likely to respond to a person's search request. This process is called "PageRank" and was the graduate school thesis of Google's founders. Some people try to fool ("spoof") this to artificially increase their Google ranking so their Web site is one of the first to be shown by Google in response to a search request, regardless of true relevance. Google responds with more sophisticated programming to prevent this. Google continues to develop better ways of assuring reliable information for people who use its services even as people try new ways to trick it.

Google is an evolving tool and some of its features may produce surprises. For example, to protect people using it, Google began warning of potentially dangerous sites that may install viruses or other malware on a computer that visits the site, giving the warning, "This site may harm your computer." This is something most people do not think about when surfing the Internet.

Yahoo!

Yahoo! has been around longer than Google and was once the leader in search engines. It still held the number two spot in search in 2010.[5] Yahoo! began as a human-reviewed and indexed directory site, with people reviewing and categorizing information by topics. This was a traditional way of choosing relevant sites for searchers. As the Internet has grown Yahoo! adapted to handle that growth with automated indexing and search programs, including the Bing search engine technology. It still has the human touch of editor-selected directories that give extra value based on the assessment of other. As Yahoo! notes, "The Yahoo! Directory is a human-created and maintained collection of Web sites organized into categories and subcategories. Yahoo! editors review these sites for potential inclusion in the Directory, and to evaluate the best place to list them."[6]

With Yahoo!'s alliance with Bing, some folks have coined the term "Bingahoo" to describe the services they offer together. But

HOW DOES GOOGLE WORK?

Google "How Does Google Work?" and look at the top results. One of them might be www.google.com/technology/pigeonrank. html. What can be said of this Web site? Is it well designed and professional? Does it appear well supported, with references and scholarly wording? Or might it be a deviously clever April Fool's joke? After reading this page, read up on Google's April Fool's joke sites at http://google.about.com/od/experimentalgoogletools/tp/aprilfools.htm.

Google has a tradition of April Fool's Internet jokes. "PigeonRank" is one of them, a pun on the PageRank system Google's creators developed in graduate school at Stanford University. Though all in fun, it shows how careful everyone must be on the Internet. More about how Google really works is available in "The Anatomy of a Large-Scale Hypertextual Web Search Engine, at http;//infolab.stanford.edu/~backrub/google.html.[25] This is the paper the founders of Google, Sergey Brin and Larry Page, wrote in college about how Google might work. Compare this to PigeonRank and how to judge which is the more reliable response.

Yahoo! still offers the human touch to those who want that extra level of analysis.

Bing and Baidu

Life brings competition. Bing is one of the newest contenders in the search engine market in the United States. Supported by Microsoft, it has vaulted into third place and has been adopted by Yahoo! as Yahoo!'s automated search system ("Bingahoo"). But it is neck-and-neck with the Chinese search engine Baidu in the world market for search. How these two engines will fare over time will be as much about politics as about commerce. Baidu, in particular, is controversial as it actively censors its content in accordance with the laws and regulations of its home country, the People's Republic of China.[7] How people respond to having their search results censored by the search service may determine its long-term prospects.

How good is a search engine if it limits what people find based on politics?

What Are the Best Power Tools for Online Search?

Deciding which search engine is the most trustworthy and helpful is difficult. Even though the searcher is supposed to evaluate the quality of the information retrieved, the ability of a search engine to pull up the best, most relevant responses in the first set of results is helpful to everyone.

If the market and popularity are good guides, then Google is the clear winner. One study showed that Google handled more than 60 percent of all searches. Yahoo! was second at 16 percent followed by MSN/WindowsLive/Bing at about 11 percent, based on the number of queries submitted to each of these search engines.[8] Another source put the global reach of Google even further ahead, with about 85 percent of the search market to Yahoo!'s 6 percent and Bing's 3 percent, based on a network of sampling Web sites that analyze visits to them that begin from the search results.[9]

References from trusted sources may be a good guide, particularly as to special types of search engines. The University of California, Berkeley Library likes Google, Yahoo!, and Exalead, for example. If business is a guide, Search Engine Watch.com's 2009 awards chose Yahoo! as producing the most relevant results, and named FanSnap.com, a live event ticket search engine, as the most innovative product. Search Engine Watch is a service for Web marketers using such sites to sell advertising. Because online searching is a dynamic field, new or better search engines may appear in the future. It is up to users to keep aware of changes and developments and assess the search engine that best suits their needs.

ANSWER ENGINES

It is about the information, not the technology. People use what gets them the best information the fastest. That's why Google is the leader in search. But people often search for specific answers to a specific question. "Answer Engines" try to refine search responses to answer questions as a teacher, friend, or otherwise living person might. These search engines let a question be posed in "natural language" as people usually ask the question and then respond with an answer. This

CAN AN ANSWER ENGINE ANSWER THE MEANING OF LIFE?

Consider how WolframAlpha, TrueKnowledge, and Answers.com responded to the following question: "What is the meaning of life?"

- WolframAlpha responded "42," noting this was the answer given in Douglas Adams's book *The Hitchhiker's Guide to the Galaxy* to just that question.
- TrueKnowledge provided a list of 14 definitions ranging from "the course of existence" to a prison term for as long as the life of the prisoner.
- Answers.com went to the brief philosophy section and discussed purpose and goals, albeit with no resolution.

This variety of results indicates that it is still each computer user's responsibility to think through the tough questions. In comparison, a Google search of the same question pulled up links to some lengthy discussions of the philosophical point, as well as cartoons about the meaning of life. Which results are better or more appropriate is up to the user to decide. Google is good for those willing to spend some time and thought to read and research what they find.

contrasts with search engines that list possibly relevant Web documents and let the searcher read through them to figure out an answer.

WolframAlpha

WolframAlpha[10] calls itself a "computational knowledge engine." The brainchild of Stephen Wolfram, it works on questions typed into its query box, regardless of whether or not that question has ever been asked before. It is particularly effective in dealing with questions relating to math and science but also handles general knowledge and social studies questions, including those that may require some calculation. But it responds best to specific questions about objective facts that are generally known, rather than opinion or philosophy questions. The site notes that it is far more than just an "online graphing calculator" but, rather, is a system to make knowledge, not just information, accessible to people.

The risk, of course, is that people might use WolframAlpha to just answer homework questions rather than using it to understand the knowledge involved and do the homework themselves. As with the responsibility to verify information, people must be responsible for their own learning.

Think how tough it is at test time when WolframAlpha is not around to help.

TrueKnowledge

TrueKnowledge[11] is another entry in the answer engine competition. A British system, it has a simple query box within which a question is typed and then an answer is given. Its goals are similar to those of WolframAlpha: to make knowledge more accessible through its system of understanding natural language questions and matching those to its ever-growing collection of facts. TrueKnowledge also relies on its community of users to provide answers to questions it may not yet have encountered.

Answers.com

Answers.com is a combination of reference site and active social network community of "answerers" who respond to questions posed by people. It adds the answers to the reference collection so when others later pose the same or similar questions those answers can be given.

These "answer engines" can be useful to help quickly access answers to specific, clearly thought-out questions. But they must not be the end of any inquiry; that still requires the user verify the answer if it is to be trusted and used.

Reliable Information on the Internet

John had a serious problem, one he did not want his parents, his friends, his teachers—or anyone else—to know about. He was very afraid of what they would say if they knew. That they'd think he was stupid or foolish. That they'd say he was careless and thoughtless. That they would make fun of him.

He knew he should see a doctor, but was worried his parents would find out. So he turned to what he thought would be a private, anonymous source of advice on what to do: the Internet.

He first tried his smartphone to see what information he could find, but it simply pulled up too much information for him to read on the screen. He then went to the computer lab in the library, going to the carrel by the rear wall and Googling for the information he thought he needed. His screen was full of responses. Many of them had advice that conflicted with what others said. He just wasn't sure what to do. Then, off to the right-hand side, he saw a response in bold that guaranteed a solution to his problem, a cure for what ailed him. This was what he needed!

John carefully read through all the information presented by the Web site. As he scrolled down he came to a section explaining that he need only send $20 to get what he needed. "Cheap enough" he thought, although he was uneasy now that he realized the Web site was trying to sell something. Reading further, he came to the Web site's description of how this "natural, fat-based, water-soluble compound" would help him.

Fat-based, water-soluble solution to all his problems?

John remembered something from his freshmen year. But what exactly was it? He vaguely remembered that was wrong, that fats and water do not mix. So a fat-based, water-soluble compound just couldn't work. Especially not for $20.

What were these people trying to pull on him?

He had saved himself $20, but realized he was back where he'd started, with no way out of what might be real trouble. Then he was really shaken. If he had believed that Web site, he would have gone down a wrong path believing he had solved his problem when it might be getting more and more serious. When it might have become too late and no treatment would have had a chance to help him.

So despite how bad things were, things could have been even worse. Now what was he going to do? Who was he going to trust before it might be too late?

Perhaps it was time to go off-line and see that doctor.

How does anyone know they can rely on information they find online? The Internet provides each person direct access to information without it passing through the filter of a librarian, a teacher, or an editor. The fundamental tool to assess, analyze, and distinguish good information from bad information is a person's good sense and reasoning.

It requires critical thinking.

Reasoning it out is the beginning, but *reliable* information is needed to begin a good solution. Is it possible to build trust online so a person does not have to conduct a constant analysis of

Internet users, particularly young people, must exercise caution and judgment when it comes to trusting information and advice found online. (*Jupiterimages*)

everything? That takes so much time, especially when time really matters. The first line of defense is the oldest: People should trust people and sources they know can be trusted. A person must find out who and what they are.

WAYS TO JUDGE RELIABILITY AND DETERMINE TRUST

There are many ways to establish that someone or some source may be trusted and to know they are reliable. It helps to apply a set of standards to information and its source before accepting it.

The Paul-Elder Model for Intellectual Standards

Sometimes standards are used to help determine whether or not something measures up or not. Dr. Richard Paul and Dr. Linda Elder set out suggested standards for reliability. They advocate for good thinking and reasoning through the Center for Critical Thinking and Moral Critique and the Foundation for Critical Thinking. Through them they set out guidelines for good, critical thinking.

Their first principle is: *People think for a purpose.* Their methods for good reasoning and critical thinking assure that purpose is met.

Critical thinking has been called "… an ability to question; to acknowledge and test previously held assumptions; to recognize ambiguity; to examine, interpret, evaluate, reason, and reflect; to make informed judgments and decisions; and to clarify, articulate, and justify positions."[1]

Critical thinking should be applied to any information found on the Internet.

The Paul-Elder Model suggests nine "dimensions" may serve as an initial checklist for determining a piece of information's intellectual value:

1. Clarity
2. Accuracy
3. Precision
4. Relevance

5. Depth
6. Breadth
7. Logic
8. Significance
9. Fairness

When reviewing something online, consider how it stands up to each of these nine measures of critical quality.

Clarity

Clarity, the clear expression of ideas, is vital. Too many discussions and claims rely on broad, vague statements that may sound good but fail to give a "clear" message of what is being said.

Accuracy and Precision

Promoting dangerous vagueness are *lack of accuracy*—facts, even minor ones, that are not quite correct—and *the lack of precision*, where "about," "around," or "close to" are used in place of a direct statement. These can be clear hints the person supplying the information either does not know what he or she is talking about or, as dangerous, they do not care. Remember that accuracy and precision are two distinct characteristics; information can have one without the other.

Relevance

The relevance of the discussion is equally vital, as a clear and accurate discussion of something irrelevant and unrelated to the issue is a waste of time. At worst, it can be used like a magician's misdirect to avoid actually discussing the issues while seeming to do so. A person, if not careful, can feel they have learned something that may be of no use to them at all.

Depth and Breadth

Depth and breadth help tell how much thought, study, research, and knowledge have gone into the discussion. Are only surface issues on a single point discussed or does the discussion embrace, or at least note, other, deeper issues? A deep, broad discussion and analysis helps assure important points are not left out or ignored. And that the person creating the information really knows the topic.

Logic

The "logic" of the discussion shows it was thought out and well considered. By setting out a path by which the reader can see the logic used to reach the conclusions, the reader can judge the validity of those conclusions and test the logic on their own. On the other hand, if discussion is "illogical," that may indicate the authors do not understand the topic, even though they want other people to accept what they say. Worst of all are those that know exactly how bad their reasoning is but do not want anyone else to catch on. Of what "significance" is the discussion? Is it "fair"? These last two standards reflect on the discussion, the people creating it, and those that choose to read it.

Significance

Significance is the importance of the discussion or the meaning it has for the reader. If the observations, facts, analysis, and conclusions do not advance the reader's understanding in some important way, then why bother? Without significance for the reader, there is no purpose to the information.

Fairness

Fairness is a kind of mirror for both the author and the reader. If the discussion acknowledges other points of view or the conflicting conclusions of others, that alerts the reader. It shows respect by letting the reader decide by knowing different points of view. It shows that the discussion was built on intellectual honesty to set out even those ideas that conflict with it.

Johns Hopkins University Sheridan Libraries

The Sheridan Libraries at Johns Hopkins University point to key tests of reliability and trustworthiness of an Internet resource, some

HOW A FALSE ONLINE POSTING LED TO DEATH THREATS

Too many people believe anything they read on the Internet.

After the terrible terrorist bombing of the Oklahoma City federal building killed hundreds of people, someone falsely posted on a bulletin board of the America Online online service provider that "Ken" was selling T-shirts celebrating the killings. Giving "Ken's" home phone number, it said to call him to get the shirts.

And he received a lot of telephone calls from angry and insulting people, including some who threatened to kill him. But he could not change his phone number as he ran a business out of his home that used that number.

And the anonymous liar continued placing false messages to call about the T-shirts for several days, inciting people to the point that "Ken" was getting an angry telephone call every two minutes.

And then a radio announcer picked up on the story and told his listeners to call "Ken", leading to more calls and death threats. He was finally given police protection because of all this. The calls began to drop off after an Oklahoma newspaper revealed the hoax and the radio station aired an apology.[2]

The liar who posted the false statements was never caught. And nobody was ever held responsible for the damage done to "Ken."

Nor is this just a unique, unfortunate event. Read more about this and other problems with online hoaxes and the damage they do in *Blown to Bits: Your Life, Liberty and Happiness After the Digital Explosion*, by Hal Abelson, Ken Ledeen and Harry Lewis of the Massachusetts Institute of Technology.[3]

If only the people who had first read the fake postings had bothered to check, an innocent person would not have been harmed.

of which require a prior knowledge of that reliability (or a willing-ness to check it out) and others that are *indicators* of reliability (that may also need to be checked out).[4] Creating, in effect, another type of checklist of reliability, Johns Hopkins recommends a Web site's information be judged based on:

- authorship
- publishing body
- point of view or bias
- referral to other sources
- verifiability
- currency

The Author

If the author of the Web site has a good reputation, that is a good indicator of reliability. An example of this might be a well-known teacher talking about a subject, such as history, politics, or science, or a critic known to the reader who comments on music, movies, or books. In either case the reader knows what to expect from the analysis presented. If the author is unknown to the reader, then there is no foundation to make a decision on trust and reliability.

The Publisher

Similarly, if the publisher of the Web site, which may or may not be the author, has a particular reputation, then a reader can apply that reputation to the reliability of the information. The publisher, like the librarian, takes on the task of assuring the information or the author is reliable enough to be trusted to post on their Web site.

For example, because anyone can become a publisher online, there have been many new Web sites that offer reviews on movies and music. Learning whether or not to trust the reviews may be difficult unless a person knows the reputation of that Web site's publisher.

Point of View or Bias

If a Web site clearly has a particular point of view or evidence of bias toward a particular subject, that should be used when judging the information presented. This can be tricky as some Web sites are honest about their point of view and some are not. Yet a reader may sometimes be able to tell from how the material is written that the Web site is "spinning" the reader toward one viewpoint rather than attempting to address different points of view.

Having a particular view on a subject is not necessarily a bad thing, and many Web sites are open and honest about their advocacy of their views. The quality of their advocacy, however, may depend on their willingness to also address competing points of view even as they disagree with them.

References

A good measure of trustworthiness is whether or not a Web site refers to other sources to support its facts and conclusions or otherwise includes information that lets a reader verify the information. Such references and verification demonstrate there is external support for the statements and conclusions and should enhance the trustworthiness of what is said.

But care is advised, as sometimes people will cite references to sources that do not actually say what they claim. Or, in some instances, do not exist at all.

Verifiability

It is important that a reader verify the references before the information can be trusted. The references cited may, in fact, not say what is claimed or can be faked. Verifiability is vital to good information, whether scholarly articles or Wikipedia entries.

Up-to-Date and Current

Lastly, the timeliness of the information presented is an important issue and a recurring problem for Web sites. Information may change quickly over time. It is risky, and may be dangerous, to rely on out-of-date information. Not all Web sites are regularly updated and many do not note when the information presented was posted or last verified. The currency of the information on a Web site must always be considered in judging reliability.

A Web site that clearly states the currency of its information shows the importance of this for a reader and helps its readers. Web sites that do not state the currency of their information require greater care, especially if embedded in the Web pages is a code that displays the current date, giving the appearance of a currency that may not be correct.

LEGAL RECOURSE

It may seem puzzling that "Ken" had little if no legal recourse for the damage done to his reputation and peace of mind from the false postings on AOL.

Well, he would have been able to sue the person who put up the false statements. The problem was that, at the time, "Ken" was not able to find out who that was and so he or she got away.

AOL, on the other hand, had the protection of a federal statute that gave it immunity from liability for what other people posted on its systems if it acted promptly to remove those postings upon notice of falsity. That federal statute was designed to protect and encourage the growth of Internet services in its early days. Internet companies, it was felt, would be afraid to provide online forums for people to exchange information if they, the companies, could be sued for what people they did not control said about others.

AOL complied with the law and, therefore, could not be held liable for the injury to "Ken." Is that fair? Should the law be changed to hold the Internet services companies liable for what people say using them? How might a change to the law change the way FaceBook or Twitter operates?

George Mason University

In her book *Helpful Hints to Help You Evaluate the Credibility of Web Resources*, Virginia Montecino, who taught at George Mason University and New Century College, suggests a reader *always* ask questions of the Web site.[5]

The questions she advises a Web site reader always ask include:

1. How do you know the author knows what they're talking about?
2. Is the author associated with a reputable organization and does that organization support the site?
3. Has the author's work ever been approved by other experts in the field, e.g., peer-reviewed publications.
4. Does the site seem to be objective or is it advocating one side or another or seem to have a preference?
5. How current is the information?
6. Are good references cited to support the claims?
7. Is the public Internet broad enough to support the information or must private services be used?
8. Is the Web site itself hosted by a legitimate and trustworthy organization, or simply a personal or advocacy site of someone?

These questions reflect the same concerns seen in the Paul-Elder critical thinking model about reliability and about opinion masquerading as fact. Like Johns Hopkins University, the focus is on the use of references to other reliable sources that can be verified.

University of California at Berkeley Library

The University of California at Berkeley Library sets out another way of verifying the trustworthiness of information.[6] The UC–Berkeley Library suggests a quick list of things a reader should do and ask when reviewing a Web site:

1. What can the Web address tell you?
2. Look around the Web page for hints

3. Look for indications of *quality* information
4. Look for support of the Web page by others
5. Review all of this together and see if it still feels reliable.

The Web Address

The Web address can tell a reader something about the trust a Web site should be given. This can start with the domain of the Web address itself, which is the last part of a Web address at the end. A Web address that ends in ".gov" or ".mil" or ".edu" is connected to a government, military, or educational institution. If a reader accounts for the inherent orientation of these institutions, the information provided will often be of high quality.

Web addresses that end in ".com" or ".net" or some other domain are selected by the Web site owner. A reader cannot infer from that domain that it is reliable, but must have some other knowledge that the Web site and its publisher are trustworthy. A Web site maintained by an enthusiastic 12-year-old may be helpful but may not be as trustworthy as one by the *New York Times*.

Hints and Quality

The page itself should offer hints or statements about the authors and their purpose in running the Web site and the quality of the information. These might include the authors' qualifications, knowledge, and experience. They can also include indications of how much effort the authors take in providing reliable information, such as how recently the page has been updated and the procedures for keeping information reliable.

On the other hand, if a Web site is set up to show the current date in a way that may mislead readers into thinking it reflects the currency of the information, caution is immediately warranted.

Support of Others

The support for the Web site by others is like having a good reputation. Other people will vouch for the quality of the Web site.

In some ways this is similar to what Google's PageRank does by counting how many other Web sites link to a particular Web site as a sign of approval. Verifying that such support is real is still needed.

All Together Now

Looking at all of these together, how does a person feel about the Web site? If there is still a nagging feeling that something's not right, then more effort should be taken to verify reliability.

FOOL ME ONCE, SHAME ON YOU . . .

The vicious Internet hoax against "Ken," which untruthfully claimed he was selling disrespectful T-shirts following the Oklahoma City bombing in 1995, was very wrong. But it was not only that an anonymous person exploited the Internet to hurt "Ken."

It is not that easy or simple.

That hoax *depended* on people *uncritically* accepting something bad that was said about him online, taking it at face value, and then deciding to "righteously" attack him based on those false accusations. Those attacks included death threats against him without ever checking to see if the story was true.

So a lot of people were fooled and turned into online tools to hurt someone who did not deserve it. Unfortunately, this was not unique.

David Mikkelson, the co-founder of hoax/legend Web site Snopes.com said, "When you're looking at truth versus gossip [online], truth doesn't stand a chance."[7] Snopes.com is built around exposing the truth behind Internet hoaxes. And they just keep coming, making it all the more important that people verify online information before acting on it.

Details of Reliability

There are many basic elements to information and how it is presented that can help users assess its reliability.

Spelling and Grammar

Even simple matters like misspellings and bad grammar can indicate the care, or lack of care, with the information. If a person did not care enough to check the spelling of what they are writing, they probably did not care enough about the accuracy of what they are posting about a particular topic.

Reliability by Association

People may be judged by their friends and associates. This applies with online information. Beyond the qualifications of the author, his or her reliability may be enhanced (or reduced) by association, such as:

- To what organizations does the author belong?
- Who supports the work of the author?
- Who opposes the work of the author?
- Who is publishing or distributing the work of the author, online or elsewhere?
- Who is publishing the online work at issue?

Objectivity—Is it Fact or Opinion Pretending to be Fact?

Several ways a Web site is written can alert a reader to possible reliability issues. Advocacy versus objectivity is one. If it appears that the author is promoting a particular idea rather than making an objective analysis, the reader knows that further investigation might be warranted. There is nothing wrong with advocating one point of view or another. It is the reader's responsibility to check the reliability of the information, though a good advocate will have the integrity not to misstate facts but present them honestly and argue skillfully from them. Integrity, however, is not a requirement for publishing on the Internet.

Courtesy

Courtesy reflects the respect a person has for others, including that person's thoughts about a particular issue, independent of whether or not a person agrees with their opinions. A courteous and respectful discussion will directly address those disagreements in a fair and reasoned manner. But if a discussion is discourteous—rude, insulting, profane—it is important to look for signs that the disrespect shown is also a disrespect for the truth or the hard work of reasoning one's way to it.

Any indication that the author is being unfair or biased toward one viewpoint or another is good grounds that extra effort is needed to check on the reliability of the claims made, but even that may not be enough.

Always Be Careful

A skillful, dishonest author is hard to catch, at least on the surface. If the information is to be relied on, and certainly if a question or "alert" is raised, the reader should look for references, see if they support the claims, and independently check out the topic for other points of view. The importance of the topic and the time available should be considered, because a person may want to pursue one of the more detailed reviews of reliability discussed.

Ultimately, each person must decide how important is it to be right and how badly things will go if it is wrong. When going to a Web site, always ask these kinds of critical questions. Consider how the answers support reliability or undermine it.

Guideposts
for Reliable Sources

Joseph helped his grandmother settle in before the new machine she had purchased. It had a huge, high-definition screen, a powerful multicore, multiprocessor system with massive memory, incredible software and exotic add-on peripherals, like TV tuners, graphics accelerators, audio mixers, and cross media burners. A lot of it was stuff he had never seen before and which she—and he—would probably never use. He was still steamed at whoever the store clerk was that had talked her into buying all this and paying probably three times more than she needed to. Yes, massively steamed. But she was very proud of her new computer that now would let her join her fellow senior citizens in all the online activities they were beginning to enjoy. And, Joseph thought, she had all this powerful equipment sold to her without any offer to show her how to use it. That's why he was there.

It was, he had to admit, nice to work with her as he showed her, step by step, the things her computer could do to take her out into the world. This was now their fourth session together as he went from the very basics of turning the machine on and using the mouse to activating programs to using those programs for the things she would like to do.

Like playing Mah-Jong, whatever that was. He'd never heard of it, but, sure enough, there was a players' site online where people could join a game and move strangely painted tiles around. Players could also chat with each other about the game, the weather, and their grandchildren.

Well, World-Of-Warcraft *was not for everyone.*

Today Joseph's grandmother wanted him to show her how to use something called "Google" to search for answers to her questions. Specifically, she wanted to use it to find answers to questions about her health and medical treatment. Some of her friends had told her about new, miracle treatments for aches and pains that "the doctors don't want us to know about" because it would hurt their business. And about all kinds of free entertainment Web sites that assured everyone they were perfectly legal.

She showed him several Web sites, all with either ".com" in their addresses or ending with some country codes he didn't recognize but knew weren't in the United States.

It startled Joseph. There was more than just pulling up Web sites to finding good information. But how could he explain that to his grandmother without being a jerk? Before he could answer, she had another question.

"Oh, Joe, can you show me how to get movies for free?"

Now what was he going to do?

Knowledge helps a person reason through whether information is reliable. Experience is a strong foundation for reason. So are trusted sources, like families, schools, libraries, trusted Internet sites, and other community institutions, all of which can help speed learning along.

A young man helps his grandfather use his computer to find information online. (*Peter Dazeley/Getty Images*)

ASSESSING THE WEB SITE ADDRESS AND "TOP LEVEL DOMAINS": TRUSTING INTERNET SITES BASED ON WHO RUNS THEM

The University of California at Berkeley Library recommends a person look at the address of the Web site to help gauge its trustworthiness. People patronize some businesses over others because of their reputation for the quality and reliability of their products and services. Sometimes even the type of business or institution can be an indicator of trustworthiness.

Similarly, there are Web sites on the Internet that may also serve as reliable resources because of the type of institution or institutions that run them. The Internet's system of naming Web sites is a guide to a certain level of reliability in the information a Web site possesses.

One of the early innovations to the Internet was a way of giving Web sites an "address" that was easy to remember. The address names follow a set of rules similar to those used to address postal mail. The address for a letter, for example, tells in what state or country the recipient is.

Like the names of countries and states on postal addresses, Internet addresses use "Top-Level Domains," like the "domains" of ancient rulers[1], to group addresses.

But instead of the grouping of physical domains like a country, the Internet Top-Level Domains ("TLDs") group Web addresses by the type of agency, organization, company, or activity at that Web site. Within these TLDs there is additional address information for a particular Web site domain.

This naming of addresses, the Domain Name System (DNS), matches the regular word addresses of Web sites to the Internet Protocol number addresses that the computers use. The original seven top-level "domains," or types of organizations, operating Web sites were designated as:

1. *.gov:* governments and government agencies, such as the United States of America (http://www.usa.gov; http://www.supremecourt.gov), California (http://www.california.gov), Kentucky (http://www.ky.gov), and others
2. *.edu:* educational organizations, such as universities, colleges, and other schools like the University of Louisville (www.louisville.edu) or the University of California at Berkeley (www.berkeley.edu.)

3. *.mil:* military organizations, such as the U.S. Army (http://www.army.mil) and the U.S. Marines (http://www.marines.mil)

4. *.net:* these are networking organizations that operate networking and Internet services, such as www.win.net, an Internet Service Provider (ISP)

5. *.org:* organizations generally, as self-selected

6. *.com:* businesses generally, as self-selected

7. *.int:* "international," for address holders that are created by international law, such as United Nations agencies and treaty-based organizations

If a site ends in the URL domain of ".gov" or ".edu" then it *may* be safe as a government or educational institution-provided resource. The ".gov" designation is reserved for federal and state governments and their agencies in the United States. The information from .gov sites tends to be reliable as most governments are careful to only post correct information, and the nature of politics is that errors will often be pointed out. But not all the time. So .gov sites are good places for accessing information, but verification is something a person should still keep in mind. Larger governments may have more resources to assure the quality of their information.

The ".edu" top-level domain designation is also an indicator of a generally reliable source of information as it is used by educational organizations such as schools. It also requires special scrutiny because not all schools have the same resources and therefore vary as to their reliability. Schools and educational institutions can range widely as to their purpose, perspective, funding, and outlook. All the things that should be considered in evaluating any Web site should be considered with any .edu site.

One advantage .edu sites may have is the reputation of the educational institution that hosts the site. For example, great universities and schools are proud of their intellectual and academic traditions and accomplishments and, over time, become known in their towns, states, regions, countries, and the world for their excellence. Those institutions usually assure that the information provided through their Web sites meets those same standards of excellence and reliability.

Sites that must be viewed with more scrutiny are ".com" and ".org" sites. These sites tend to be self-selecting as to their designation across a huge range of activities. In other words, any person or organization can choose one of these types of domains. The top-level domain name tells little about the site.

If the site is known to be reliable, to one degree or another, a person may take that into account in using the information. Major newspapers, for example, register their on-line editions as ".com" sites; those online sites are as reliable as the print version of the newspaper. But as anyone can register a ".com" or a ".org" Web site, the accuracy and reliability of the contents of the site rest with that person.

Countries may choose to add their national abbreviations as the top-level domain for Web sites within them. ".ca" is the top-level domain for Canada. ".uk" is the top-level domain for the United Kingdom. ".cn" is the TLD for the People's Republic of China while ".ch" is the TLD for Switzerland.

New top-level domains are being added for more categories of Web domains. ".mobi" is for mobile device Web domains while ".museum" is for museums, ".info" is for information services, ".biz" is for businesses and ".jobs" is for employment sites. The Internet Assigned Names Authority (IANA) lists them all, from ".ac" (Ascension Island) to ".zw" (Zimbabwe.)[2]

Always be careful with what is typed; sometimes people will register near-matches to popular and respected Web sites, hoping to catch users who make a mistake in entering a Web address or searching, and lure them to advertising or, worse, misleading or dangerous sites. For example, entering www.newyorktimes.com retrieves the online version of the *New York Times*, a respected national American newspaper. But a simple typo of entering www.newyorktime.com (no "s") at one time redirected the search to a Web site advertising time-share sales.

ANYONE CAN OWN
A WEB SITE DOMAIN

To see how easy it is to own a domain and Web site name, visit one of the domain registrations sites listed below. Check to see available Web site names and how much they cost to register and host.

- GoDaddy: http://www.godaddy.com
- Register.Com: http://www.register.com
- Network Solutions: http://www.networksolutions.com

Visiting www.GoDaddy.com, a popular Web site domain name registration and hosting site, the Web site name "I-Always-Tell-The-Truth-Online.com" was available in September 2011 for a bargain registration price of only $9.99 per year! Notice all the other new possibilities for domain names that cost a great deal less; "I-Always-Tell-The-Truth-Online.info" is a mere $1.99 to own for a year.

To make things even more interesting, there are a number of new basic categories of types of Web site being proposed. These are designed to help users and Web site operators focus on particular subject areas. While this will help with classifying information, these new address names do not assure the reliability of the information on the Web sites.[3]

SCHOOLS

As with all the other knowledge and skills they hope to teach, teachers can help students with their ability to find and use good information. Their formal teaching mission often leads students to more structured and effective development of the skills needed to identify credible information on the Internet. Using online research skills in the context of school classes can also help students to develop both knowledge of locations of good information and critical analysis of that information.

LIBRARIES

A library's professional staff can help guide researchers to good resources, including online materials. The same is true for small libraries and school libraries.

The level of engagement of a particular library in supporting online resources is important. The greater the commitment to online research, the more likely library resources and staff will be able to help guide and direct someone to good online information. The library itself may maintain a list of trusted Web sites for online information. Using and trusting these Web sites is like using and trusting the books found in a library.[4]

The extent to which a library's online site can assist varies with the policies and resources of that particular library. Some libraries provide Web site links to trusted open Internet sites. Some provide access to private databases of information, although they may require library membership and entry of a library card number and password to access the site.

Libraries may subscribe to and pay for proprietary, private business data services that offer access to online information. Part of the justification for the fees is that the information is more reliable. Depending on the particular library, those fee-based information services may be available to use through the library, either at its physical location or through the library's online site.

For example, the Louisville Free Public Library entered the digital era with extensive Internet and other online resources for the community and provides free access to online research tools for the public from journals, reference resources, archived newspapers and other sources not yet freely available over the Internet. These private (proprietary) resources often come with some assurances of reliability not found in all freely available Internet resources.

COMMUNITY INSTITUTIONS

Communities may be sources about trusted information, including online. The friendships that evolve through Facebook, for example, represent an informal community of friends. Associations that can develop around Facebook groups may also represent people of like interests sharing them together. These communities may be sources of information or references to information.

THE LIBRARY CARD—A LICENSE TO LEARN, REGARDLESS OF AGE

Most libraries offer varying degrees of online information support to the people of their communities and beyond. Some examples are:

- Los Angeles Public Library—Los Angeles, http://www.lapl.org and http://databases.lapl.org
- Chicago Public Library—Chicago, http://www.chipublib.org and http://www.chipublib.org/cplbooksmovies/research/online_research.php
- British Library—London, http://www.bl.uk
- New York Public Library—New York, http://www.nypl.org
- Louisville Free Public Library—Louisville, Kentucky, http://www.lfpl.org

See what special, reliable information services other libraries provide.

Family members can often be helpful in determining whether information on the Internet is reliable. (*Peter Cade/Getty Images*)

But the relationships in online communities may lack a level of familiarity or proximity that people are more familiar with in the physical world. Because of that, trust and reliability are sometimes more difficult to ensure, so a person using online communities must be vigilant. In both physical and online communities it is especially true that trust is often built over time. Each new encounter with a community member whose information or advice turns out to be good and helpful builds more trust. That is how communities grow and thrive, just like their members.

FAMILIES

The rise of the digital world and the Internet has been so swift that sometimes the youngest members of a family may have the best skills for working with information online. But the important issue here is more than just using Google or texting at the speed of light; it is about the trustworthiness of information. Family members may be able to use their experiences over many years, good or bad, to give guidance as to what seems to be reliable and trustworthy. Turning to family members still may be a good place to start when searching out good sources, or locations, for reliable Internet information.

While the older generation can teach the younger what they have learned through time and experience, especially about trusting others, the younger generation can teach the older about this new, unprecedented world of instant information.

All of these guides may help, to one degree or another. As with everything else, they must be used carefully and critically.

Where to Find
Information Online
About News, Health,
and Jobs

A bad experience makes people very hesitant to do something like it again. "Once burned, twice shy," is an old saying. Sonia had been fooled by some online jerk who had posted a sharp-looking Web site that was massively wrong about the supposedly "free" music she could download by her favorite musicians. And it had cost her a lot of money to deal with.

Now she began her research with a list of sites recommended by her teacher. A former criminal prosecutor who had left his job to teach high school, he seemed to really worry that his students would screw up. Sonia wondered why anyone would leave a great job as a criminal prosecutor to teach, anywhere. Was he hiding from thugs or the Mafia? When she complained about how stupid some people were on the Internet, putting up trash as fact, though, he'd stopped her and asked what she wanted to do. After she explained she was interested in setting up an online shop to sell music she and her friends produced, he'd nodded and said he would check out some things for her.

He did, and then e-mailed her a list a list of things to look for with the Web sites that he said she could trust. Some things were specific Web sites on which she might rely as to the legal issues involved (especially copyright), good and legal ways to advertise (no spam) and getting paid for her work. Others were groups of Web sites that he said were more trustworthy than others. Above all else, though, he said no matter how much a Web site seemed reliable, always remember, as every lawyer must, to "Trust but Verify!" He told Sonia that if she was just having fun on the Web, fine, but if she was making an important decision, she had to check out any advice from someone she did not know.

Whatever, Sonia thought. Perhaps he had spent too much time dealing with cops and criminals, murderers, and liars. But maybe that was why he might know what he was talking about. Maybe that was what she had to do. After all, not checking out information she had found online was how she'd gotten burned in the first place.

Sonia took the list. And turned on her computer.

On a day-to-day basis, people often seek information on the news, health, and jobs.

The kind of information people seek on the Internet is seemingly endless. But these three areas encompass among the most popular topics where reliability is important. Web sites linked to and associated with reliable off-line sources can offer secure, trustworthy information online. If the off-line reputation is good, the online reputation should be, too.

THE NEWS

Newspapers, television broadcasters, and news aggregators have spent years building readership and viewership based on their reputation for reliability. All major news outlets—newspapers, magazines, television, radio—have online versions of their news services. They want to preserve their reputations for timeliness and reliability to assure people keep reading. Many respected and reliable news organizations in the United States and Europe provide information online without charge. So good, reliable information on current events can be found on those Web sites.

Some of those that offer a high level of reliability are:

- The Associated Press—A leading news aggregator providing current news as it develops, http://hosted.ap.org/specials/bluepage.html
- The American Broadcasting Company online news site— One of the leading television news organizations in the United States, http://abcnews.go.com
- Reuters News Service—A Europe-based news aggregator providing a different perspective on world events, http://www.reuters.com

The Web sites of Ongo, the *New York Times*, the *Washington Post*, and Gannett are displayed on a computer screen. Ongo, a start-up founded in 2011, aggregates news and information from multiple publications for a monthly fee. (*Daniel Acker/Bloomberg via Getty Images*)

- The *Guardian* newspaper—One of Britain's leading news-papers, also often offers a different view of the news, http://www.guardian.co.uk
- The *Wall Street Journal*—The *Wall Street Journal* is a leading source of financial and general news reporting in the United States, http://online.wsj.com
- The *New York Times*—Another source of general news in the United States, http://www.nytimes.com

All of these primary news Web sites use their own editorial and review policies to ensure the reliability of the news they report. They may still be in error, but their reputations for excellence in news reportage have been built on competence and thoroughness such that their information is highly trustworthy.

Online and Specialty News Sites

There are specialty information service providers and information sites that exist only online and have developed strong readerships. The trustworthiness of each of these sites should be independently evaluated, however, that may be made easier by the reputations of those news sites for reliable information.

Arstechnica.com is a technology information Web site that describes and prides itself on good analysis of the "art of technology."[1] In discussing digital devices, electronic games, physics, computing, or technology law and policy, Arstechnica does not shy away from showing the opinions of its authors. But it requires its authors and editors to give rigorous support for any analysis presented as well as clearly stating opinion versus fact. It has both free and pay access; a paid subscription permits access to subscriber-only forums for more detailed discussions of issues.

Wired.com[2] is the online version of *Wired* magazine, another news source specializing in technology with high standards for its articles. Slashdot.org[3] is a purely online service started by a small crew of highly proficient technical folks that wanted a news service on technology matters of interest to them, such as Linux, open source software, free speech and games. As they describe it: "News for Nerds, Stuff that Matters." Slashdot commentaries usually include a link to a source that lets the reader verify and read further about the subject discussed there.

The reader has the responsibility to verify the information; a good online news source has the integrity to make that verification easier.

News Clipping Services

Some Web sites, such as Google News, offer a shortcut to finding individual news sources by collecting news sites and posting them on a single site. The reader must still judge the reliability of the particular article from a particular source, but this saves time. The clipping service may also choose to only collect information from Web sites they deem reliable, further helping the reader.

In the case of Google News, short news article titles and taglines are pulled from many different online sources and presented together with primary information from other Web sites.[4] News stories are categorized into various topical areas, ranging from top stories and most popular to business, science and technology, entertainment, health, and sports. Google News lets users set up preferences to create personalized news Web pages that follow the topics of interest to them.

Unlike the primary news Web sites mentioned earlier, Google News does not use its editorial review and standards to assure the reliability of the particular information presented. That reliability rests on the trustworthiness of the sources linked to the Google News Web page.

The Google News site on July 1, 2011, 9:30 A.M. EDT had six "Top Stories" from 10 different sources ranging from the *Wall Street Journal* to Bloomberg News. Its World section had 20 stories on Syria, Venezuela, Thailand, Cameroon, China, and other countries from 43 sources, ranging from the *New York Times* to the Chinese Xinhua to Al-Jazeera to Ha'aretz.

Another type of clipping service is Arts and Letters Daily, more of a Web site magazine clipping and linking service that uses references from people as to what it should feature.[5] With the more personal touch, ALDaily has links and short descriptions on articles across a broad spectrum of human knowledge. It is host to a huge number of links to online sites for selected newspapers, magazines, book reviews, columns, blogs, and various other information sources. This list is a useful compilation of resources but, as with anything, anyone using them must consider the perspective that may have led to their inclusion in the listings and why others may have been excluded.

Asserting itself to be "one of America's best independent political Web sites, RealClearPolitics "culls and publishes the best commentary, news, polling data, and links to important resources from all points of the political compass."[6] These and other sites offer convenient access to online news resources, some of which may not be easily found directly.

A Comment on Comments on News Stories

Many of these online news sources take advantage of the interactive nature of the Internet to give readers the opportunity to comment on news stories and share their views. This can engage people in the news and provide an opportunity for additional analysis and commentary about stories in the news. But these comments do not go through the editorial and fact-checking process expected of news stories and may only reflect the opinions of the people making the comments. As such, a reader should never assume the comments are as reliable and accurate as the news story on which they are made.

HEALTH

Online health information is a delicate area. With it someone can help save a life or possibly destroy one. It is with good reason that advertisements for new medicines almost always warn people to see their doctor before using them. Choosing trustworthy health sites

IS INFORMATION ON THE INTERNET FOREVER?

The Internet Archive, www.archive.org. is a nonprofit project that works to store as much digital information as it can to help researchers and historians, now and in the future, recover information about today.[7] One consequence of this is that even if someone deletes information from a Web page or a blog, that information might still be available through the Internet Archive.

One tool for recovering old and deleted Internet material is the Wayback Machine, a searchable collection of more than 150 billion Web pages going back to 1996.[8] The Wayback Machine can find Web materials people thought they had erased long ago. Another tool is Google Groups, which provides access to archives of the Usenet discussion groups back to 1981. That archive covers more than 800 million messages going back to the beginnings of the Internet.

So when someone says something on the Internet is gone, they should remember it might be there for a long, long time. And there may be little they can do to remove it.

and using them properly often requires extra special effort. Consider the results of a Google search for "trusted health sites" run on November 11, 2009. Many have "trust" in their titles, but that is not enough. It is necessary to consider what each link shows.

Note first that at the top right side of the results screen may be the word *Ads* in light gray text. These responses are there at the top of the first set of results because they *paid* to be placed there. Rather than being judged by the Google search engine to be the best results as compared to all other Web sites, and given the top placement on the results page, these Web sites pay Google to appear there as part of the advertising program Google offers. This does not mean these sites are not trustworthy, but it means a person should be aware they are a commercial business seeking customers, and favorable placement in Google's search results.

Other results do not appear to be paid advertising but results Google deems most responsive to the search request. But are they reliable? How would a person know? Results of a Google search for "health" included the following responses. Of the six shown here, four are .com domains, one is a .gov, and one is an .edu domain. Look at what they say:

Healthcentral.com—Trusted, Reliable and Up To Date Health . . . Healthcentral.com is one of the most trusted sources of medical information and up to date news and contains a doctor-approved health encyclopedia of . . . www.healthcentral.com/

Symptoms	Find Dr. Dean's Radio Program
Health Library	Contact Us
About Us	About Dr. Dean
Drug Library	People's Pharmacy

More results from healthcentral.com »

Trusted Health Products
That's where Trusted Health Products differs. We formulate our products to be recognized by the body as food and to be totally consumed by the body for your . . . www.trustedhealthproducts. com/

MedlinePlus Health Information from the National Library of Medicine
MedlinePlus Trusted Health Information for You. Search Terms . . . Local health services, libraries, organizations, international sites, and more www.nlm.nih.gov/medlineplus/

Psych Central—Trusted information in mental health and psychology reliable, trusted information & self-help support communities for over 14 years. . . . Member of Everyday Health Network · Time 50 Best Web sites —2008. . . psychcentral.com/

Disclaimer—HealthyOntario.com provides trusted health . . . HealthyOntario.com is a trusted online resource for a variety of health, . . .There may be Web sites linked to and from this site that are operated or . . . www.healthyontario.com/Disclaimer.aspx —

trusted sites
Begin your search with a health information portal like MedlinePlus. A health information portal is a Web site with documents and links that are. . . www.livinghealthy.peoria.uic.edu/ sites.html

Even in these descriptions someone searching for good health information might trust some more than others. Beginning with some of the principles discussed above, someone searching might first select a .gov or .edu site and then choose one associated with a good reputation. The National Institutes of Health and the U.S. National Library of Medicine online health site, MedlinePlus, would meet these tests.[9]

The MedlinePlus site offers general information on hundreds of health topics, drugs and medicines, and on medical conditions and terms. It offers much of this in over 40 languages, so it is a service for others around the world as well as people in the United States that have not yet mastered English. It provides a beginning directory for doctors, dentists, and hospitals as well as access to other kinds of local resources, such as clinics and advising offices. If someone really wants to know what exactly the surgery they are thinking about is like, videos and interactive slideshows are available for viewing. Though for some people, viewing these videos may be a rather gruesome experience. MedlinePlus keeps a directory of health organizations by topic and name so someone searching for a specific topic can go directly to organizations specializing in that particular area of medicine and health.[10] These organizations include federal government agencies, state agencies, and organizations and non-governmental organizations and foundations such as the Kaiser Family Foundation.

The topic listings on MedlinePlus are extensive. For "A" topics alone the listings range from AIDS and acne to autism and autonomic nervous system disorders. At its most extensive, MedlinePlus offers access to huge databases of articles and medical information, though these are primarily written for medical professionals. Nonetheless, it puts in the hands of anyone willing to search what may be crucial information on health and wellness.

This does not mean other health sites cannot be helpful. Some are easier to use than MedlinePlus and may help users more quickly find exactly the help they need. But verification of the reliability of the information is always going to be needed.

This is such a concern that a nongovernmental organization, the Health on the Net Foundation (HON Foundation), was formed to offer some standards for Web site operators regarding the reliability of their health information.[11] Yet some question how well this works: The HON Foundation notes that it is easy for a dishonest Web site operator to place a fake HON certification logo on its Web site. So, again, it falls back on the person searching to verify reliability.

JOBS

In today's world, finding a job nearly always requires access to online resources. Fewer and fewer businesses advertise in newspapers and even when they do, they will also often post online information. The reliability issue for job postings is mostly one of currentness: An old job opening still posted on the Web site could already be filled. Personal safety and fraud can also be issues if a particular job posting is not from a reputable company but instead from an individual posing as a business trying to arrange an "interview" in a strange or isolated location or gather personal information from those who respond. Or just trying to trick an "application fee" out of a hopeful job seeker.

Key Web sites for job searches largely depend on the nature of the job and the employer. For instance, USAJOBS is the Web site for the U.S. Office of Personnel Management. It links to jobs available in the U.S. government both domestically and around the world.[12] State and local governments often maintain their own job Web sites. Each state government Web site can be searched to find its available job openings. The state of Kentucky maintains its government job postings at the Kentucky Personnel Cabinet.[13] Job postings for the Commonwealth of Virginia are listed on its Virginia Jobs site.[14]

Private businesses and organizations present special concerns for someone looking for a job. Many post job openings on their company Web sites, but more and more, companies are also choosing to post on large national job Web sites, such as Careerbuilder.com and Monster.com. Still others post through local, national, and trade organizations. *Forbes* magazine conducted an analysis of job Web sites by number of visits. Although this may show popularity, does it necessarily equal reliability in offering a fair chance at a good job? "The Best Way to Find (And Fill) a Job Online"[15] notes the following as the sites most visited:

- Careerbuilder.com
- Hotjobs.yahoo.com
- Monster.com
- Simplyhired.com
- Indeed.com
- Usajobs.com
- Job.com
- About.com
- Snagajob.com
- Kenexa.com

To assure the timeliest and most complete information about jobs posting, a careful search on any of these sites would not be complete without going directly to the Web sites of businesses offering the employment opportunity. This will provide valuable information about the job and work environment not detailed in an online job offering.

Employers appreciate someone who seems to care enough about working for them that she or he is willing to learn about the business, even before the job is offered.

And reviewing a company's Web site also gives a job seeker the opportunity to learn more about the potential employer. This "due diligence" research on a possible employer can help someone make sure the job they are applying for is the job they want. This is the sort of advanced information about an employer that, in the past, could only be discovered if a person knew someone who worked for that employer or was familiar with their reputation.

Together this can help someone find the job that person truly wants and with which they will be satisfied. The online world can help, but only if a person is careful with what they do with the information they find.

Internet Risks
to Watch For

John was trembling. Everybody got fooled or ripped off at one time or another from scams and thieves on the Internet. But he'd never thought he'd be sitting at the table across from a very grim, very serious federal agent. They were waiting for his mother's attorney to arrive. The feds had agreed to that. He had spoken on the telephone to his mother's—now his—lawyer, and the lawyer said that he must not say anything until he arrived.

"It's O.K., though, right, this is just a juvenile court matter that will go away if I apologize, right?" he had said.

The lawyer didn't say anything for what seemed like a long, long time. Then he responded: "No, John, the federal system is different. There is no juvenile court. You would be charged and tried before the U.S. District Court, just like a drug lord. While you are under 18, this will be a confidential case that takes into consideration your juvenile status. But if you turn 18 during the prosecution you will be treated just like any adult charged with a felony."

But it was them, John thought, it was those people he had met online that asked him to help them. He didn't know they were doing anything wrong when he let them use his computers for online file sharing. He wouldn't hurt anyone or commit a crime and didn't think anyone else he knew would.

He had trusted them, but, now, he had to admit he didn't really know them. And when he shared his computer's storage and Internet services with them, they used it to distribute sexually explicit materials, including illegal materials an online police investigator had found and traced back to his computer and his home.

"Just don't say anything, John," the lawyer said, "I'll be there soon."

John leaned back in his chair and tried hard not to look as scared as he felt.

"How could they have done this to me?"

Many people believe there is no danger in using the Internet or from the people they meet there. That's not always the case.

There is information supporting and describing the use of illegal drugs, discussing anorexia nervosa, bulimia nervosa, and suicide as good things and offering how-to guides for these and other kinds of conduct that may destroy health and life. If someone reads this information uncritically they may end up hurting themselves or others. Countries such as the United Kingdom and France are among those to have highlighted the dangers of so-called pro-anorexia ("ana" for short) sites that seek to help readers maintain an anorexic disorder and risk starving themselves to death.[1]

Sometimes a person can be deceived by a relationship they strike up with someone in an online community. Paula Bonhomme became friends with "Jesse James," someone she met through an online community of fans of the *Deadwood* television show. Putting aside the suspicious name, this "friend" eventually became her "boyfriend" with whom she planned to live and for whom she ultimately spent $10,000 on gifts.[2] But "Jesse" was a fictional, online person created by another of Paula's online friends, Janna St. James. St. James also

This Web site advertising discount designer boots was shut down by authorities when customers either received counterfeits or nothing at all. (*Press Association via Getty Images*)

created up to 20 other fictional, online persons to fill out the story of "Jesse's" life until, alas, he "died." A lawsuit is proceeding to see if St. James will be liable to Bonhomme for the money she paid and the emotional distress she claims to have suffered from this affair.

BUYING, SELLING—BAD INFORMATION AND MONEY DECISIONS

Knowledge is power. And money. So people should be concerned about the reliability of information on the Internet when they spend their money based on it. It is possible for someone to lose everything they paid or invested based on bad online advice.

In cases of outright thievery, people have paid for a new automobile just to see the seller disappear, taking their money but not

THE SMOKESCREEN GAME

Melissa Hathaway is concerned about information reliability and security, especially with computer and Internet systems. She served in the administration of President Barack Obama as acting senior director for cyberspace in the National Security Council and in the administration of George W. Bush as cyber coordination executive and director of the Joint Interagency Cyber Task Force in the Office of the Director of National Intelligence. Her work led to cybersecurity becoming a presidential priority for the United States. So would she, as a top authority on cybersecurity in the county, ever consider that a game might be a good way to prepare people for the risks with unreliable or deceptive information online?

Ms. Hathaway suggests it might very well be and points to one online game as a new, "out-of-the-box" approach to information security and online reliability: the SmokeScreen Game. The SmokeScreen Game (http://www.smokescreengame.com) is a British project to let students test life online through social media and their interactions with others in the electronic world. The SmokeScreen Game looks at issues like online rumors, misinformation, careless hatred, and even criminal and terrorist activity.

Hathaway firmly believes that public awareness about current real-world problems in this area is key to success, because everyone who goes online needs to take responsibility for what they do with what they find there.

leaving a car. More difficult cases involve getting something that is not quite what was promised, like meeting an online dog breeder at a local fast food place to pay $1,500 for a healthy pedigreed puppy only to learn weeks later that it is sick and dying. Some people puff things up online to convince others to pay more, like bragging that the stock of a company is a great buy when they are trying to inflate

Melissa Hathaway, former acting senior director for cyberspace for the National Security Council, gives a keynote address at a conference. (*AP Photo/ Marcio Jose Sanchez*)

the stock price so they can sell *their* stock at a huge profit. And then run and hide.

Ignorance can be just as damaging, even though the person giving out erroneous information believes it to be true. It is just like the dangers of ignorant and misinformed health information online, except it is a person's financial health and well-being at risk.

People who earn their livings by providing reliable information to others are also worried about bad financial information online. The Dow Jones Corporation is a financial news provider whose reputation depends on the accuracy of its information. It is the publisher of financial newspapers the *Wall Street Journal* and *Barrons*. Dow Jones teamed up with the Special Libraries Association, a group of information professionals in business, government, and education, to study what impact on business decisions, if any, bad or misleading information on the Internet had.[3] Those decisions might relate to products or services to buy, investments to make or even people to hire or not hire.

Dow Jones went on to detail, in summary, the special areas of concern regarding bad information on the Internet.[4] The worst type of bad information was *opinion disguised as fact,* with the biggest cost the wasted time spent verifying and checking on claims and facts. Biased sources were also a top type of bad information along with factual errors that over half of those surveyed noted. Interestingly, the group most likely not to realize they were relying on bad information were business people, perhaps because of their inexperience with the Internet. But in second place came students, so even growing up with the Internet does not assure protection from bad information. And the worst sources of information were blogs and social media sites, though general Web sites were not far behind.

The scariest fact was that 41 percent, or more than two out of five people, ended up making bad decisions based on bad Internet information.

If that is applied to health information, then there is a real danger to people's health. According to the Pew Internet and American

Life Project, 8 of 10 people using the Internet look for health information.[5]

A summary of the Dow Jones Bad Info survey responses listed the top three types of bad information found, the top three dangers bad information created, the three groups most likely to be deceived by bad information, and the top three sources of bad information. Those were:

Top three types of bad information:
- Opinion disguised as fact: 72 percent
- Biased sources: 69 percent
- Factual errors or misstatements: 59 percent

Top three dangers of bad information:
- Wasted time double-checking facts: 69 percent
- Wasted time vetting sources: 49 percent
- Bad decisions made based on bad information: 41 percent

Top three groups most likely to fall prey:
- Business people: 36 percent
- Students: 28 percent
- Inexperienced/new researchers: 26 percent

Top three bad information sources:
- Blogs and other social media sites: 61 percent
- General Web sites: 57 percent
- Marketing materials: 35 percent

This is clearly a risk of hurting many people.

BAD INFORMATION TO CHEAT: FIGHTING INTERNET FRAUD

The U.S. Federal Bureau of Investigation, the U.S. Secret Service, the U.S. Federal Trade Commission (FTC), and many others are trying to stop online theft, but it is very difficult. The FTC is the leading agency fighting online scams. The scams range from Internet auctions and credit card fraud to pyramid schemes and the sale of "proven" health products that do not work. Electronic commerce has exploded in the United States. Amazon.com, Dell.com, and eBay.com are practically household terms. When communicating online or paying for goods online using a credit card, everyone must be careful to avoid scams or fraud intended to steal a person's identity or money and perhaps ruin that person's reputation and credit history. This is called identity theft. While this activity may be illegal, it is not easy to prosecute when the criminals have taken all the money and live on the other side of the world. These criminal deceptions come in many forms: The best way to avoid them is to use good sense and reason.

It is as though the Internet has given a vast new life to the 100-year-old Spanish Prisoner scam that asks for help (and money) for a rich person in trouble overseas (wrongly imprisoned) in exchange for the promise of wealth. But the money disappears, as does the person asking for help.[6] The current scam is criminals posing as former officials in Nigeria, Sierra Leone, Russia, or a number of other countries who claim to need help transferring money they have stolen from the government to overseas bank accounts. All they need is the bank account number and transfer codes for an overseas account. With these in hand, they then proceed to empty the account. These scams come online, in the mail, and are particularly egregious when aimed at the elderly.

ADVICE FROM THE INTERNET CRIME COMPLAINT CENTER, FBI, NW3C, AND THE FTC

To combat national (and international) problems with fraud on the Internet, several federal agencies have set up resources and services to help protect people using the Internet. To help those victimized by cybercrime, the Internet Crime Complaint Center was established to take complaints from people who have been defrauded. It is a partnership of the Federal Bureau of Investigation and the National White Collar Crime Center (NW3C) and takes complaints not only of Internet fraud but of hacking, Internet extortion, threats and harassment, identity theft, and other offenses.

Filing a Complaint with IC3

IC3 (http://www.ic3.gov) describes how to file a complaint of a cybercrime with them:

> IC3 accepts online Internet crime complaints from either the person who believes they were defrauded or from a third party to the complainant. We can best process your complaint if we receive accurate and complete information from you. Therefore, we request that you provide the following information when filing a complaint:
>
> - Your name
> - Your mailing address
> - Your telephone number
> - The name, address, telephone number, and Web address, if available, of the individual or organization you believe defrauded you.
> - Specific details on how, why, and when you believe you were defrauded.
> - Any other relevant information you believe is necessary to support your complaint.

With this information in hand, a person can go to the online complaint site from a link at the bottom of the www.ic3.gov Web page or directly at http://www.ic3.gov/complaint/default.aspx to begin the filing of a cybercrime complaint.

IC3 also gives advice to avoid being a victim (http://www.ic3.gov/preventiontips.aspx). That list covers tips on avoiding these types of online fraud schemes:

- auction fraud
- counterfeit cashier's check
- credit card fraud
- debt elimination
- DHL/UPS
- employment/business opportunities
- escrow services fraud
- identity theft
- Internet extortion

- investment fraud
- lotteries
- Nigerian letter or "419"
- phishing/spoofing
- Ponzi/pyramid
- reshipping
- spam
- third-party receiver of funds

THE FTC

The U.S. Federal Trade Commission cites the top scams that have come to their attention, noting the "bait" (what lures people into the scam), the "catch" (the trick the criminals use), and the "safety net" (the technique a person should use to avoid being tricked and defrauded by the scam). The FTC offers this list of scams ("Dot Cons") describing the way an online user may be tricked ("The Bait"), how that person may be cheated ("The Catch"), and ways to critically analyze and detect that someone may be trying to cheat "(The Safety Net"). The following is excerpted from "Facts for Consumers: Dot Cons, U.S. Federal Trade Commission":[7]

Internet Auctions

- *The Bait:* Shop in a "virtual marketplace" that offers a huge selection of products at great deals.
- *The Catch:* After sending their money, consumers say they have received an item that is less valuable than promised or worse yet, nothing at all.
- *The Safety Net:* When bidding through an Internet auction, particularly for a valuable item, check out the seller and insist on paying with a credit card or using an escrow service.

Credit Card Fraud

- *The Bait:* Surf the Internet and view adult images online for free, just for sharing your credit card number to prove you're over 18.

CONSUMER NEWS
REPORTER

**Foods that Fuel
Weight Loss**
*"Super foods are becoming a real
source in the battle to fight fat..."*

Acai Berry Diet Exposed: Miracle Diet or Scam?

Tuesday, January 04, 2011

As part of a new series, "Diet Trends: A look at America's Top Diets" we examine consumer tips for dieting during a recession

» **RELATED VIDEOS**

**Super foods: How to
Balance your Body.**

 **Consumer Reports**

Julia investigates the
Acai Berry diet to find out
for herself if this super
diet works.

Acai berries are the latest weight loss fad. These
so called Super Foods that you take as a
supplement to lose weight have been getting a
lot of international attention. And like you have
probably already seen; they are all over the
internet in blogs and success stories of people
who have apparently used the pills and lost a
ton of weight. But we here at News 6 are a little
skeptical and aren't sure that we've seen any
real proof that these pills work for weight loss.
So we decided to put these products to the test.
What better way to find out the truth than to
conduct our own study?

To get started, I volunteered to be the guinea
pig. I applied for a bottle of the LeanSpa Acai.
While there are ton's of acai berry ads online, LeanSpa Acai is one of
the most credible and trustworthy suppliers on the market. It included
the Free trial of the product and it did not try to fool me into agreeing
to additional hidden offers. Another reason why I chose LeanSpa Acai
is because it is the most concentrated and purest acai products on the
market. This would give me the most accurate results for my test.

Here is what LeanSpa Acai claimed on their website...

- 4 Times More Weight Loss Than Diet And Exercise
- Boosts Energy
- Rich in Antioxidants
- Promotes Cardiovascular and Digestive Health

Were pretty skeptical, but wanted to find out for ourselves if this
product could actually do everything that it claimed. Most of the
success stories talk about combining Acai berry with colon cleansing
products to achieve maximum weight loss. I decided to do the same.
The idea behind combining the products is that while the Acai Berry
encourages weight loss and increases energy, the colon cleanse helps
rid your body of toxins and allows your body to work and burn
calories more efficiently. I chose Get Slim Cleanse to test.

Here is what Get Slim Cleanse claimed on their website...

- Helps Eliminate Bad Toxins that have Built Up Over the Years
- Removes 'Sludge' from the Walls of the Colon
- Helps Get Rid of Gas and Bloating
- Helps to Regulate the Metabolism

And the Get Slim Cleanse, like the Acai Berry, had a Free trial with a
100% satisfaction guarantee and had no hidden offers.

Putting Acai to the Test

Both the LeanSpa Acai and Get Slim Cleanse arrived within 4 days of
having placed my order online for the Free trials.

The bottles I received held a month's worth of pills which worked out
perfect as I was to follow the supplement routine for 4 weeks time

Health and Diet writer, Julia Millar of the
News 6 team recently put the Acai Diet to the
test. She spent four weeks testing the effects
of America's Newest Superfood combined with
a Colon Cleanse to see for ourselves what this
diet was all about. And, the results were
surprising

She lost 25lbs in 4 weeks.

The benefits of the Acai berry diet beat all of
our initial skepticism. We found the diet not
only with weight loss, but it seemed to boost
energy levels, and also helped Julia sleep
better and to wakeup more rested.

Step 1:

First get **LeanSpa Acai**
Use our exclusive promo code "LEAN195" to
get $1.99 shipping!

Step 2:

Then get **Get Slim Cleanse**
Use our exclusive promo code "news6" to get
$1.50 shipping!

*This is key. Use both for results like Julia

Offers Expire On Wednesday, January 5, 2010

Network Reviews:

 ABC News Calls Acai Berry
A Superfood! Many world-
class athletes have started
using Acai berry products
as part of their personal
training regimen.
- ABC News

Change your approach to living
better. Why it is important to learn
how to balance your diet.

**The Real Dangers of
having a Toxic Colon**

Special CBS new report on the
importance of colon health. Why it's
important to remove toxins from your
colon.

» **ADVERTISEMENTS**

Get a
Celebrity
Looking
Body Today!

An image provided by the Federal Trade Commission shows a screen
shot of a fake news Web site used to promote acai berry weight-loss
products. (*AP Photo/ Federal Trade Commission*)

- *The Catch:* Consumers say that fraudulent promoters have
  used their credit card numbers to run up charges on their
  cards.
- *The Safety Net:* Share credit card information only when
  buying from a company you trust Dispute unauthorized

charges on your credit card bill by complaining to the bank that issued the card. Federal law limits your liability to $50 in charges if your card is misused.

Travel and Vacation

- *The Bait:* Get a luxurious trip with lots of "extras" at a bargain-basement price.
- *The Catch:* Consumers say some companies deliver lower-quality accommodations and services than they have advertised or no trip at all. Others have been hit with hidden charges or additional requirements after they have paid.
- *The Safety Net:* Get references on any travel company before doing business with it. Then, get details of the trip in writing, including the cancellation policy, before signing on.

Business Opportunities

- *The Bait:* Be your own boss and earn big bucks.
- *The Catch:* Taken in by promises about potential earnings, many consumers have invested in a "biz op" that turned out to be a "biz flop." There was no evidence to back up the earnings claims.
- *The Safety Net:* Talk to other people who started businesses through the same company, get all the promises in writing, and study the proposed contract carefully before signing. Get an attorney or an accountant to take a look at it, too.

This is just a partial list that highlights the most common ways bad people try to cheat others, especially people new to the online world who do not know the risks But these cheats are very creative and spend much energy and time thinking up new ways to steal. It is important to test for the reliability and trustworthiness of anyone trying to sell something on the Internet. It is vital if what is being sold can affect someone's health and/or financial well-being.

The U.S. Federal Trade Commission observes that it may not be possible to avoid all such fraudulent offers online, but "prudence pays." In "Facts for Consumers: Dot Cons," it suggests these analysis tips to help consumers analyze what is presented and avoid getting caught by a fake offer:[8]

- Be wary of extravagant claims about performance or earnings potential. Get all promises in writing and review them carefully before making a payment or signing a contract.
- Read the fine print and all relevant links. Fraudulent promoters sometimes bury the disclosures they are not anxious to share by putting them in teeny-tiny type or in a place where they are unlikely to be seen.
- Look for a privacy policy. If there is none or it is difficult to understand, do business elsewhere.
- Be skeptical of any company that does not clearly state its name, street address, and telephone number. Check it out with the local Better Business Bureau, consumer protection office, or state attorney general.

These tips do not work by themselves. Before accepting any online offer, a person must analyze the offer in light of these and other factors to minimize the risk of being a victim of bad online commerce.

For videos, interactive games, and more information on protecting yourself, check OnGuard Online, a collaborative effort on the part of the FTC, U.S. Department of Commerce, U.S. Department of Homeland Security, the Internal Revenue Service, U.S. Department of Justice's Office of Justice Programs, and U.S. Securities and Exchange Commission.[9] The site focuses on the broad area of computer and information security, which is important for every computer and digital device use.

And should someone end up a victim of an online scam, they can file an online complaint with the FTC at www.ftc.gov or call toll-free, 1-877-FTC-HELP (1-877-382-4357); TTY: 1-866-653-4261.

PERSONAL SAFETY IS AT STAKE

This is a much bigger issue than online seller and buyer fraud. The problem of reliable information on the Internet extends to activity that attempts to harvest personal information to do other kinds of damage, such as identity fraud and identity theft. The sites presenting the greatest risk are social media, where someone may be lured or tricked into revealing much more information about themselves than they should. These are some of the tips the FTC suggests for exchanging information and socializing safely online (excerpted from "Social Networking Sites: Safety Tips for Tweens and Teens," U.S. Federal Trade Commission[10]); everyone has heard them before, but they are worth repeating:

- Think about how different sites work before deciding to join a site.
- Think about keeping some control over the information you post.
- Keep your information to yourself. Do not post your full name, Social Security number, address, phone number, or bank and credit card account numbers—and do not post other people's information, either.
- Make sure your screen name does not say too much about you.
- Post only information that you are comfortable with others seeing—and knowing—about you.
- Remember that once you post information online, you cannot take it back.
- Consider not posting your photo.
- Flirting with strangers online could have serious consequences.
- Be wary if a new online friend wants to meet you in person.

The greatness of the Internet is that it brings people closer to all the great information in the world. The risk is that it also brings people closer to the bad. So it is critical to always be vigilant and apply good reason to determine and separate the good from the bad.

8

What Is Right in the Online World

Justin and his friends could not believe what they heard in class. People who said horrible things about a soldier killed in battle and his family in an online Web site had been sued by a grieving parent. And the court had let them go! Did that mean that the horrible things they said were true? That just couldn't be. But it must be, if they could hurt that soldier's family so badly without being held responsible.

So Justin, alone and quietly, did something he had never done before. He asked a teacher after school what was going on. He asked a really old fellow who taught physics. The other students said he worked them too hard but was decent enough.

"How may I help you?" the teacher asked him. Justin told him his concerns. He wanted to know how could anyone say such terrible things and get away with it unless they were true. Strangely, the teacher leaned back in his chair looking even older than when Justin stepped into his room.

"Son, that is a really difficult issue at the core of our country's being. It's part of the bargain made for the freedoms for which our

ancestors came here. That freedom is built on the free exchange of ideas and belief. In exchange, we let some fools have their say."

"So I can say whatever I want about these people or anyone else on my Facebook page, right?" Justin said.

"No, you can't, because our forefathers' bargain is still a complex legal question and it is easy to get in trouble saying the wrong thing. As well as morally wrong. And I said some fools, not all fools, can get away with saying bad things.

"And don't forget the bargain, which helps protect people who just say things others just don't like. Nobody likes criticism, especially when it's true. Shoot, son, in Pennsylvania they locked up an honors student for posting a spoof MySpace page to ridicule an assistant principal at her high school."

Justin shook his head. "So there's no protection from this stuff, it's just a crazy world out there?"

"No, there's plenty to protect you. Starting with your own ability to think. That you even questioned this whole mess shows you are thinking. Don't stop.

"But you can't stop here with just this piece of outrage. At some point you'll have to decide if you want to step up and challenge the statements with which you disagree, using reason and facts. And that won't be easy. Or pleasant. The greater the lie, the more time and practice the liar spends on it and the more people end up supporting it. So the harder it is to challenge deceit. But somebody has to do it."

Justin stared for a moment and then thanked him and headed back down the corridor. He heard the teacher say, "And Justin, think about taking a tougher class or two. It's good preparation. For everyone's future, not just yours."

Information can hurt. Can people who put up information that injures others be held legally accountable for it? The answer, in the best American lawyer tradition, is, "Sometimes." When a person goes to a restaurant, they do not worry about the safety of the food. They naturally assume that it will be good and safe (regardless of its healthfulness). When a person drives a car, they assume that it will be safe, the wheels will stay on it, the engine will not catch on fire, and it will perform as cars are generally expected to. That is because this country, as do many countries, has a system of product safety inspections that help assure the safety of what people eat and drive and wear.

There is also an extensive legal system of personal liability that holds people responsible if their products or their conduct hurt other people. That also encourages safe food and safe cars. But when it comes to information, especially information online, it can be a whole different matter. Holding people responsible for the information they put out can be a complex and difficult legal matter, especially in the United States and other countries where freedom of speech is given a high priority.

There is little law enforcement can do about bad information on the Internet unless it is connected to a criminal scheme like fraud. That means that the ways in which society assures that hamburgers and T-shirts and music players are safe do not always apply to information. This is because, in part, people do not always *know* if what they are saying is right or wrong. It is what they believe to be correct. People disagree about lots of things. If everyone was afraid of being arrested for what they said no one would say anything.

Only in special circumstances can someone be punished for bad information, and then only with difficulty. And sometimes it is illegal to put up good information. The laws regarding property rights in information are complicated and create risks for people who do not mean to do harm.

To make this situation even more complicated, what can be posted online may be legal in one country but may be illegal in another. The Internet has suddenly made everyone who uses it a citizen of the world. A person might not find out they broke the law of another country until they go on a trip abroad and are arrested for something they said or did with a Web site or on a blog or chat site.

Saudi women board a taxi in Riyadh, Saudi Arabia. In May 2011, a group of Saudi women started a Facebook page urging authorities to lift the ban on driving for women. The group posted a video on the site of a woman behind the wheel in a Saudi city. The page was removed after more than 12,000 people indicated their support for its call for women drivers to take to the streets in a mass drive on June 17, 2011. (*AP Photo/Hassan Anmar*)

For example, four people in Lebanon were arrested for allegedly slandering the president of Lebanon on a Facebook page.[1] A Saudi woman was arrested for posting YouTube videos of her driving in Saudi Arabia, where it is illegal for women to drive automobiles. People who operated online gaming sites that are legal in their country of operation but not in the United States have been arrested when changing planes on international flights that connected through U.S. airports. People can be caught in this even for something posted on their Web site that was visited by people in another country. It can be a mess that did not really exist until the international information system of the Internet connected everybody everywhere.

People have different ideas about the importance of free speech in American culture and society. For example, the most recent controversy that went all the way to the Supreme Court was whether or not California could make it a crime to sell or rent what California considered to be a violent video game to a minor; the Supreme Court said "No," that free speech rights applied to software and in this case could not be restricted by government. In earlier cases the Supreme Court upheld the right of students to state their opposition to war, of people to espouse unpopular views, and of citizens to anonymously criticize public officials.

Though free speech is controversial, it is a core part of life in a free country. People who say something false or hurtful about someone can be sued in court, but in the United States, it is unlikely someone will wind up in jail solely for speech that is false, erroneous, or offensive. They could still go to jail if that speech was meant to harass, defraud, or encourage criminal or violent acts, but those are intentional acts meant to harm in violation of criminal statutes.

However, in many other countries, people can be jailed for their words alone.

It is important to understand at least the broad outlines of the new and evolving laws of information in the Internet world to know what is protected and what is not.

A customer holds a *Grand Theft Auto* video game displayed at Best Buy in Mountain View, California. In a June 2011 decision, the Supreme Court ruled that California cannot ban the rental or sale of violent video games to children. (*AP Photo/Pakuma*)

SHOULD THERE BE MORE LAWS ON BAD INFORMATION?

This is a difficult issue. Maurice Schellekens and Corien Prins in The Netherlands were concerned about the unreliability of health information on the Internet and the lack of accountability. Being lawyers and teachers, they wondered why, when people are held responsible when they makes mistakes in almost all other areas of activity they are not held responsible for some things they say on the Internet.

Schellekens and Prins asked these questions:

1. Should there be laws about the reliability of information?
2. If yes, what kind of laws might help improve the reliability of information?
3. What other results, intended and unintended, might there be if people are required to assure reliability in what they say?

BAD INFORMATION—REALITY CHECK

If they give me bad information, I'll sue them!
Not in the United States; generally, under U.S. law, people cannot sue over "bad information" unless fraud is involved. Surprisingly, in this area ignorance is a defense.

If they lie about me, I'll sue them!
Not so easily in the United States; generally, under U.S. law, it is more difficult to sue over lies and false statements that are "published" over the Internet; the legal costs are significant and the plaintiff has to find out just who the "liars" are before going after them. In the country of Turkey, though, the political leader there has sued hundreds of people for criticizing him in ways he asserts are false.

Generally, in the United States there is no liability for giving out inaccurate information if there is no intent to trick someone. The exception is when there is some special relationship between the person giving out the information and the person receiving and relying on it. Examples of this might be a doctor and a patient or a lawyer and a client.

This is partly due to considerations of the First Amendment's protections for freedom of speech. There are also practical concerns about how potential liability for anything said anywhere might choke the free exchange of ideas. That is why broadcasters, newspapers, magazines and, yes, Internet publishers can usually get away with no liability for things they say. And in Europe the situation is even less clear as to what law, if any, may apply.

Schellekens and Prins suggested changing the law to hold information providers liable. Possible liability might encourage more people to start out assuring the quality of their information. It would allow for "enforcement" later to make people correct misleading information.

There are risks. Usually liability develops only after someone is hurt. Until people are held liable on a regular basis, like in car accidents, there will not be much incentive for good information. And working out the issues with freedom of speech—differences of opinion, the costs of defending lawsuits worldwide, and the differences in laws worldwide—might be practically impossible.

Again what happens when a student in the United States posts a blog about political activity on the other side of the world in China that results in an arrest warrant in China? Or a student comments on a writer in England only to be sued for money damages in London?

These are situations people currently face under existing laws. The *New York Times*, in a 2009 editorial "Libel Tourism," called upon the U.S. Congress[2] to follow the lead of New York and Illinois and adopt laws prohibiting people from trying to enforce in the United States judgments they get from foreign courts regarding free speech and libel issues. But that is not the law yet. That editorial notes that an American author wrote about a Saudi Arabian businessman financing terrorism. Rather than sue her in the United States, the businessman chose to sue her in Great Britain, where a few copies were sold; since the author did not come to court, the British court ruled against her for $200,000.

People can be sued far from home where items they have posted online could be seen in other states and countries.

A student could probably ignore those legal actions for the moment, but if one day in the future, having forgotten about those law cases, that student visited China or England, he or she might be in for an unpleasant surprise.

So extending this to laws enforceable everywhere raises difficult questions. People should not be hurt by others, but should freedom of speech be curtailed to address this problem?[3]

What precisely is legal on the Internet can also be the subject of lots of bad information on the Internet. People who do not know what they are talking about or who are pushing their own interests can easily mislead others. The problem of bad or useless legal advice on the Internet is just another example of the general problem of reliable information. The issue of legal advice on the Internet has spawned a parody Web site about legal advice on the Internet, which advises that its legal advice should be printed out, crumpled up, and thrown away immediately.[4]

But "Free Legal Advice Ask A Lawyer Parody" keeps the word "Parody" in big letters at the top, just in case someone might actually believe what they say.

Regardless of what other people say or do, using computers and the Internet to hurt others is wrong and a potential cybercrime. Cybercrime includes "traditional" criminal activity that specifically exploits unique aspects of computers. Traditional criminal activity is misconduct that has been criminal well before the advent of computers, even if not common. These traditional crimes relate to the misuse of information and might as easily be described as "information crimes." What distinguishes their application from those in the pre-computer and Internet days is the ease with which they may now be committed and the expansion of the number

WHOSE LAW APPLIES TO ONLINE CONDUCT

Most people live their lives in one place where one set of laws by one government apply. But the Internet has made it much easier to be a citizen of the world.

The Internet covers the world. Because of this, there are three general groups that have the right and power to legally punish conduct involving the Internet under a concept called "jurisdiction."

Those are

- the country where the computer an individual is using is located
- the country where the Web site, chat room, or social media site the individual is accessing is located and all communication via e-mail, Skype, or chat is received
- the countries through which an individual's message passes.

Each of the countries where these activities happen could have their police enforce laws against improper use of the internet. If a country did not wish to do so, then it would be difficult, even impossible, for another country to try to enforce the law. Jurisdiction usually ends at the physical border of a country, even as the Internet ignores those boundaries. It is a vexing problem for regulation of the Internet.

of possible offenders, particularly those who may not see their conduct as wrong. The hallmark example of this is copyright violation using computers and networks.

CRIMINAL COPYRIGHT AND CIVIL COPYRIGHT VIOLATIONS

Do not be fooled by people who encourage others to share files without a thought. Things are different in the information world, but there are some common elements to consider.

Copyright deals with the *rights* to use information but, though centuries old, has not been part of common experience in the way that the possession of physical property, and its theft, have been. Copyright crime is not a *traditional* theft in that a person does not physically "take" any property. If a person has a copyright on a song, when someone copies that song the copyright owner still has 1) the copyright to it and 2) their copy of the song. But it may still be illegal because the person making the unauthorized copy is *infringing* on the statutory rights of the song owner's copyright, and *that* may be a crime and grounds to sue in civil court.

With the advent of personal computers and their ability to copy electronic files and media, anyone with a computer could easily and cheaply copy and distribute anything in electronic form. But not everyone has experience with copyright infringement as misconduct. The copyright holder does not seem to lose any property. And often people copy from materials they purchased and may assume the right to copy.

They are wrong.

Copyright is one of the strangest areas of law as it deals with information and knowledge and the expressions of those things. Efforts to express this in clear legal terms can be difficult.

One way is to look at "copyright" not simply as property but as a special collection of "rights," just like a person has a right to keep some things private or the right not to talk to the police.

To make things more confusing, the language of copyright law does not talk in terms of violating rights. It talks about "infringing" and the "infringement" of rights, words that seem much less serious than the violations of theft or burglary or robbery.

Copyright includes almost all created expressions of information except that copied or taken in part from someone else.

A screen shot shows an image of the Nickelodeon character SpongeBob SquarePants on the YouTube Web site. Nickelodeon owner Viacom Inc. sued YouTube and its parent company, Google Inc., in March 2007, seeking more than $1 billion in damages on claims of widespread copyright infringement. In a major victory for Google, a judge threw out Viacom's lawsuit in June 2010. (*AP Photo*)

The U.S. copyright statute is complicated, but the basic structure of copyright is that the owner of the copyright has certain exclusive rights in copyrighted works[5] that only he or she can say others can use, subject to some complex exceptions.[6] The critical rights relevant to computers, networks and cybercrime are exclusive control of 1) reproduction (copying) and 2) distribution of the copyrighted work. This matches perfectly with the power of computers, especially over the Internet, to copy and transmit electronic information.

Copyright and criminal copyright laws have increased penalties for violations over the past 10 years as publishing interests, particularly in computer software, music, and motion pictures, have sought to curb piracy of their intellectual property.

Most copyright violations are handled as civil lawsuits for the payment of money, but criminal prosecutions are now possible for unauthorized copyright infringement where, for example, music or video files valued at more than $1,000 (retail) are copied or distributed during any 180-day period, and video or music files are copied, distributed, or otherwise misused for private financial gain, including the receipt of other copyrighted video or music files. The threat of criminal prosecution has not been fully used except in cases of massive infringement, usually for some type of financial gain. But the possibility exists for the extensive use of criminal enforcement, particularly where this conduct can be used to obtain search warrants for the seizure and search of computers.

This is one of many ways bad advice about what can or cannot be done legally on the Internet can cause harm.

HOW WILL THIS ALL END?

There is no end to the pursuit of knowledge. Everybody wants to know what's going on all the time. Far back 2,500 years ago, one great leader in the debate over how people should live and think said, "All people, *by their nature*, desire to know."[7]

The challenge is how to know right from wrong. That has never been easy. Just as many people try to help others know the truth, others do the opposite. Sometimes that is out of malice but it is mostly out of ignorance.

Will people let others decide for them? Or will they choose to decide for themselves?

No one can ever stop watching out for dangers in information and knowledge: to themselves, to those they love, to that upon which they can rely and depend.

That is the way it is in all areas of life, online and off. Each person's challenge is to learn how to act wisely and safely in this new world of information. There are many areas and examples of risk to people in the online world. Sadly, some of those examples are of how some people have cruelly hurt others. Consider those practices discussed here to protect people from the information crisis and risk in the great new world of Internet knowledge. Think how people can work together to protect and help each other. Some still need to learn to be mature online. People must still be willing to use their minds and their reason, to discern the truth.

People will always want to learn things about the world. Leonardo da Vinci expressed this as, "The desire to know is natural to good men." And according to the New Testament, Christ more universally put it that, "You shall know the truth, and the truth shall set you free."[8] But each person must be responsible and use his or her mind to know the truth and separate it from the ignorance and lies in the online world. Each person has the strength to do it.

Each person can do it and will.

● ● ● CHRONOLOGY ● ● ●

3100 B.C. Use of numbers and symbols in Sumer.[1]

A.D. 600-900(?) Block printing developed in China.

A.D. 1440 Gutenberg perfects and deploys movable type that permits affordable printing of books and papers.

1733 First "social" library open for subscribers in the United States.

1833 First public library open to all in the United States opens in Peterborough, New Hampshire.

1835 Electrical telegraph first built in the United States.

1875 Alexander Graham Bell invents the telephone in the United States.

1893 Principles of radio demonstrated to the public by Nikola Tesla.

1929 An all-electronic television is developed (as opposed to the earlier mechanical spinning-wheel television).

1945 Vannevar Bush describes a machine to create and follow links from one document to a cited document, a precursor to hyperlinks.

1955 First pocket-sized, transistor radio sold commercially.

1962 Joseph Carl Robnett Licklider of the Massachusetts Institute of Technology (MIT) describes a worldwide network of computers he dubs "Galactic Network." He later becomes the head of the Defense Advanced Research Projects Agency (DARPA).

The first computer game, "Spacewar!," was created at MIT.[2]

Mid-1960s E-mail use begins on local networks.

1968 DARPA requests price quotes to begin development of the ARPANET network between University of California–Los Angeles and Stanford University to test how a wide-area network (WAN) might allow text and file communication over wide distances.

1976   The Apple I personal computer appears on April Fool's Day.[3]

1980   The U.S. military adopts the Internet TCP/IP electronic communication rules for its systems and contractors follow suit.

1981   The IBM Personal Computer (PC) is released.[4]

1985   The U.S. NSFNET program begins; it conditions funding for Internet systems on opening those systems to all users across all disciplines and using the TCP/IP rules.

1989   Physicist Tim Berners-Lee, worried about the loss of information at the giant European CERN physics laboratory, due to the huge amount, proposes creating a "web" of information between research notes using "hypertext."[5] [6]

1989   America Online (AOL) offers Internet services for nontechnical users.

1990   Work begins on a "hypertext" system and Berners-Lee coins the term *World Wide Web.*

1992–1993   The "World Wide Web" component of the Internet begins to spread to universities and research institutions.

1994   "Realizing the Information Future: The Internet and Beyond"[7] is published by the National Research Council, Computer Science and Telecommunications Board outlining the future of the Internet as a system open to all users, all types of services, all types of network providers and to ongoing change and innovation.

1994   Yahoo! starts out from a trailer on the Stanford University campus as "Jerry and David's Guide to the World Wide Web," a directory of Web sites.[8]

1995   The Federal Networking Council (FNC) formally defines "the Internet."[9]

Internet is privatized and its expansion becomes the responsibility of private telecommunications companies, as with telephone communications.

1996 The search engine that would become Google is launched and run out of a dormitory room at Stanford University.[10]

1998 Google moves to a garage in Menlo Park, California.

1999 Google moves to nicer offices.

2001 Google offers search of images, indexes 3 billion Web pages, and is available in 26 languages.

2002 Google offers Google News.

2005 Facebook is released commercially; Google offers Google Maps and Google Earth.

2006 Twitter is released commercially; Google offers Book Search and Patent Search.

2007 iPhone is released; Google offers StreetView viewing services.

2009 *140 Characters: A Style Guide for the Short Form* is released by Dom Samgolla, one of Twitter's developers.

2010 Facebook has over 500 million users.[11]

2011 11.1 billion searches were performed via Google Sites in March, 2011; 2.7 billion were performed via Yahoo! Sites and 2.4 billion via Microsoft.[12]

People in Spain ask that information collected and stored in Google about them be removed, claiming "a right to be forgotten."[13]

ENDNOTES

CHAPTER 1

1. Reno v. American Civil Liberties Union, 117 S.CT. 2329, 138 L.ED.2D 874 (1997).

2. Paul Scullard, Clare Peacock, and Patrick Davies, "Googling Children's Health: Reliability of Medical Advice on the Internet," *Archives of Diseases in Childhood* 95, 8 (August 2010): 580–582 doi.

3. MasterBase Glossary of Technology Terms, www.en.masterbase.com/support/glossary.asp (Accessed March 20, 2011).

4. Peter Mell, and Tim Grance, "The NIST Definition of Cloud Computing," http://csrc.nist.gov/publications/drafts/800-145/Draft-SP-800-145_cloud-definition.pdf (Accessed June 18, 2011).

5. Nicholas Carr, "Is Google Making Us Stupid?" *The Atlantic Magazine*, July/August 2008, http://www.theatlantic.com/magazine/archive/2008/07/is-google-making-us-stupid/6868 (Accessed June 18, 2011).

6. Keith Hampton, Lauren Goulet, Lee Rainie, Kristen Purcell, "Social Networking Sites and Our Lives," http://www.pewinternet.org/Reports/2011/Technology-and-social-networks.aspx (Accessed June 19, 2011).

7. David Pogue, "At Snopes.com, Rumors Are Held Up to the Light," *New York Times*, July 15, 2010.

8. National Public Radio "Mom-And-Pop Site Busts The Web's Biggest Myths," *All Things Considered*, http://www.npr.org/templates/story/story.php?storyId=124958817 (Posted March 20, 2010).

CHAPTER 2

1. "Wiki Skirmishes: Online Profiles of Politicians Have Become Battlegrounds for Both Spin Doctors and Mischief Makers," Governing.Com, http://www.governing.com/topics/politics/Wiki-Skirmishes.html (Accessed June 18, 2011).

2. Nikko Dizon, "Gov't Loses Case for Citing Wikipedia, *Philippine Daily Inquirer*," Inquirer.net, http://newsinfo.inquirer.net/inquirerheadlines/nation/view/20100829-289336/Govt-loses-case-for-citing-Wikipedia (Accessed March 20, 2011).

3. Ibid.

4. *USA v. Sypher*, United States District Court for the Western District of Kentucky, Case No. 3:09-cr-00085-CRS, Docket # 223, Memorandum Opinion of Judge Charles Simpson, p. 6, footnote 4.

5. *USA v. Sypher*, United States District Court for the Western District of Kentucky, Case No. 3:09-cr-00085-CRS, Docket # 228-1, Supplemental Motion/Notice of Additional Judicial Misconduct, pp. 4–7.

6. *USA v. Sypher*, United States District Court for the Western District of Kentucky, Case No. 3:09-cr-00085-CRS, Docket # 231, Order Denying Renewed Motion to Disqualify, of Judge Charles Simpson

7. *USA v. Sypher*, United States District Court for the Western District of Kentucky, Case No. 3:09-cr-00085-CRS, Docket # 239, Judgment

8. "Wikipedia: About," Wikipedia.org, http://en.wikipedia.org/wiki/Wikipedia:About (Accessed March 28, 2011).

9. "Researching With Wikipedia," Wikipedia.org, http://en.wikipedia.org/wiki/Wikipedia:Researching_with_Wikipedia (Accessed March 20, 2011).

10. Ibid.

11. "Wikipedia," Wikipedia.org, http://en.wikipedia.org/wiki/Wikipedia (Accessed April 16, 2011).

12. Giles, Jim "Internet Encyclopedias Go Head to Head". *Nature* 438 (7070): 900–901, December, 2005, http://www.nature.com/nature/journal/v438/n7070/full/438900a.html (accessed June 30, 2011)

13. Larry Sanger, "Why Wikipedia Must Jettison Its Anti-Elitism," Kuro5hin.org, http://www.kuro5hin.org/story/2004/12/30/142458/25 (Accessed April 16, 2011).

CHAPTER 3

1. Bob Carter, "Keep a Weather Eye Open," The *Courier Mail*, Queensland, November 16, 2005; Billy Simpson, "Billy Simpson's Column," *Belfast Telegraph*, April 17, 2000.

2. Google, "Google Search Basics," Google.com, http://www.google.com/support/websearch/bin/answer.py?answer=136861

(Accessed March 20, 2011); Yahoo, "Yahoo! Advanced Search," Yahoo.com, http://search.yahoo.com/web/advanced (Accessed March 20, 2011).

3. StatCounter Browser Stats for May 10–11, 2011, http://gs.statcounter.com (Accessed June 19, 2011).

4. Sergey Brin and Larry Page, "The Anatomy of a Large-Scale Hypertextual Web Search Engine," Stanford University, http://infolab.stanford.edu/~backrub/google.html (Accessed April 18, 2011).

5. comScore, "comScore Releases February 2011 U.S. Search Engine Rankings," comScore.com http://www.comscore.com/Press_Events/Press_Releases/2011/3/comScore_Releases_February_2011_U.S._Search_Engine_Rankings (Accessed April 18, 2011).

6. Yahoo!, "How Does The Yahoo! Directory Differ from Yahoo! Search," Yahoo.com, http://help.yahoo.com/l/us/yahoo/directory/basics/basics-03.html;_ylt=AhoZiFaUWn9_7W2kTRMNEZpGkiN4 (Accessed March 21, 2011).

7. *China Digital Times*, "Baidu's Internal Monitoring and Censorship Document Leaked (1) (Updated)," Chinadigitaltimes.net, http://chinadigitaltimes.net/2009/04/baidus-internal-monitoring-and-censorship-document-leaked (Accessed March 21, 2011).

8. Nielsen Company, "Top U.S. Online Search Providers: November 2009," NielsenWire, http://

blog.nielsen.com/nielsenwire/
online_mobile/top-u-s-online-
search-providers-novem-
ber-2009/(Accessed September
13, 2011)

9. NetMarketShare, "Search Engine
Market Share," Netmarket-
share.com, http://marketshare.
hitslink.com/search-engine-
market-share.aspx?qprid=4
(Accessed March 21, 2011).

10. WolframAlpha, http://www.
wolframalpha.com (Accessed
March 21, 2011).

11. TrueKnowledge, http://www.
trueknowledge.com (Accessed
March 21, 2011).

CHAPTER 4

1. Ideas To Action, "What is Critical
Thinking?" University of Louisville (Citing Hullfish & Smith,
1961; Ennis, 1962; Ruggiero,
1975; Scriven, 1976; Hallet,
1984; Kitchener, 1986; Pas-
carella & Terenzini, 1991; Mines
et al., 1990; Halpern, 1996; Paul
& Elder, 2001; Petress, 2004;
Holyoak & Morrison, 2005)
http://louisville.edu/ideasto
action/what/critical-thinking/
what-is-critical-thinking (Accessed April 16, 2011).

2. *Zeran v. America Online, Inc.*, 129
F.3d 327, 328 (4th Cir. 1997).

3. Hal Abelson, Ken Ledeen, and
Harry Lewis, *Blown to Bits: Your
Life, Liberty and Happiness After
the Digital Explosion.* (Boston:
Addison-Wesley Publishing,
2008).

4. Elizabeth Kirk, "Information and
Its Counterfeits: Propaganda,
Misinformation and Disinfor-
mation," The Sheridan Librar-

ies, Johns Hopkins University,
http://www.library.jhu.edu/
researchhelp/general/evaluat-
ing/counterfeit.html (Accessed
April 16, 2011).

5. Virginia Montecino, "Criteria
to Evaluate the Credibility of
WWW Resources," George
Mason University, http://
mason.gmu.edu/~montecin/
web-eval-sites.htm (Accessed
April 16, 2011).

6. University of California at Berkeley
Library, "Evaluating Web Pages:
Techniques to Apply & Ques-
tions to Ask," University of Cali-
fornia at Berkeley, http://www.
lib.berkeley.edu/TeachingLib/
Guides/Internet/Evaluate.html
(Accessed April 16, 2011).

7. Stephanie Salter, "Chain E-mail
… Like That's a Bad Thing"
Edmondsun.com. http://www.
edmondsun.com/opinion/
x537287050/Chain-e-mail-like-
that-s-a-bad-thing (Posted April
28, 2010).

CHAPTER 5

1. Internet Corporation for Assigned Names and Numbers,
"Top-Level Domains (gTLSs),"
http://www.icann.org/en/tlds
(Accessed April 16, 2011).

2. Internet Assigned Names Authority, "TLD List," http://data.iana.
org/TLD/tlds-alpha-by-domain.
txt (Accessed March 23, 2011).

3. Internet Corporation for Assigned Names and Numbers
(ICANN) "ICANN-Accredited
Registrars," http://www.icann.
org/en/registrars/accredited-list.
html (Accessed April 16, 2011).

4. Thomas Dowling, "Libweb: Library Servers via WWW," Webjunction.org, http://lists.webjunction.org/libweb (Accessed April 16, 2011).

CHAPTER 6

1. Ars Technica, "About Us," Arstechnica.com, http://arstechnica.com/site/about-ars-technica.ars (Accessed April 16, 2011).

2. *Wired* magazine, http://www.wired.com (Accessed April 16, 2011).

3. Slashdot, "About Slashdot," Slashdot.org, http://slashdot.org/faq/slashmeta.shtml (Accessed April 16, 2011).

4. Google News, http://news.google.com (Accessed April 16, 2011).

5. Arts and Letters Daily, http://www.aldaily.com (Accessed April 16, 2011).

6. RealClearPolitics, http://www.realclearpolitics.com (Accessed April 16, 2011).

7. The Internet Archive, http://www.archive.org (Accessed April 18, 2011).

8. The Internet Archive, "Wayback Machine," http://www.archive.org/web/web.php (Accessed April 18, 2011).

9. MedlinePlus, "Medline Plus: Trusted Health Information for You," National Library of Medicine, http://www.nlm.nih.gov/medlineplus (Accessed April 16, 2011).

10. MedlinePlus, "Collection of Organizations Providing Health Information Arranged by Topic," National Library of Medicine, http://www.nlm.nih.gov/medlineplus/organizations/orgbytopic_a.html (Accessed April 16, 2011).

11. Health on the Net Foundation, https://www.hon.ch (Accessed April 16, 2011).

12. USAJOBS, "Working For America," http://www.usajobs.gov (Accessed April 16, 2011).

13. Kentucky Personnel Cabinet, "Career Opportunities," Kentucky.gov, http://personnel.ky.gov/employment (Accessed April 16, 2011).

14. Virginia Jobs, "The Commonwealth of Virginia's Employment and Resource Center," Virginia.gov, http://jobs.virginia.gov (Accessed April 17, 2011).

15. Miriam Marcus, "The Best Way To Find (And Fill) A Job Online," Forbes.com, http://www.forbes.com/2009/05/26/job-seeking-websites-entrepreneurs-human-resources-monster.html (Accessed April 18, 2011).

CHAPTER 7

1. Nate Anderson, "Psychiatrists Want Crackdown on Pro-Anorexia Web sites," Ars Technica.com, http://arstechnica.com/tech-policy/news/2009/09/psychiatrists-crack-down-on-pro-ana-eating-disorder-sites.ars (Accessed April 17, 2011).

2. Jacqui Cheng, "Woman Spends $10K on Fake Boyfriend: Cyberbulling or 419 Scam?" Ars Technica.com, http://arstechnica.com/tech-policy/news/2011/03/lori-drew-redux-woman-faces-fraud-claim-

thanks-to-fake-boyfriend-plot.
ars (Accessed April 17, 2011).

3. Dow Jones and the Special
   Libraries Association, "Bad info:
   Unreliable Information from
   Web Leads Many Businesses to
   Bad Decisions, Missed Oppor-
   tunities According to Survey,"
   Dowjones.com, http://www.
   dowjones.com/pressroom/
   SMPRs/BadInfoSurvey1.html
   (Accessed April 17, 2011).

4. Ibid.

5. Susannah Fox, "The Social Life
   of Health Information 2011,"
   Pew Internet and American Life
   Project, http://www.pewinter
   net.org/~/media//Files/Reports/
   2011/PIP_Social_Life_of_
   Health_Info.pdf (Accessed May
   23, 2011).

6. Celtnet Frauds and Scams,
   "Welcome to the Celnet
   Internet Fraud Page for the
   Spanish Prisoner Con," Celnet.
   org, http://www.celtnet.org.
   uk/internet-scams/spanish-
   prisoner.php (Accessed April
   17, 2011).

7. U.S. Federal Trade Commission,
   "Dot Cons" Federal Trade Commission, http://www.ftc.gov/
   bcp/edu/pubs/consumer/tech/
   tec09.shtm (Accessed April 17,
   2011).

8. Ibid.

9. OnGuard Online, http://www.
   onguardonline.gov (Accessed
   April 17, 2011).

10. U.S. Federal Trade Commission,
    "Social Networking Sites:
    Safety Tips for Tweens and
    Teens," Federal Trade Commis-
    sion, http://www.ftc.gov/bcp/
    edu/pubs/consumer/tech/tec14.

shtm (Accessed April 17,
2011).

CHAPTER 8

1. Babylon and Beyond, "Lebanon:
   Arrests Over Alleged Facebook
   Slander of the President," *Los
   Angeles Times*, July 29, 2010,
   http://latimesblogs.latimes.
   com/babylonbeyond/2010/07/
   lebanon-arrests-over-alleged-
   facebook-slander-of-president.
   html (Accessed May 23, 2011).

2. "Libel Tourism," *New York Times*,
   May 25, 2009, http://www.
   nytimes.com/2009/05/26/
   opinion/26tue2.html (Accessed
   May 23, 2011).

3. Maurice Schellekens and Corien
   Prins, "Unreliable Information
   on the Internet: A Challenging
   Dilemma for the Law," *Journal
   of Information, Communication,
   and Ethics in Society* 4, 1 (January 2006): 49-59.

4. Freelegaladviceaskalawyerparody.
   com, "Free Legal Advice Ask
   A Lawyer Parody," http://www.
   freelegaladviceaskalawyerpar
   ody.com/about-us.htm (Accessed March 25, 2011).

5. 17 USCS § 106 (U.S.).

6. 17 USCS §§ 107 through 122 (U.S.)

7. Aristotle, W.D. Ross, trans.,
   Metaphysics, Internet Classics
   Archive, http://classics.mit.edu/
   Aristotle/metaphysics.1.i.html
   (Accessed April 17, 2011).

8. *Holy Bible*, New International
   Version, John 8:32, Zondervan
   (1973).

CHRONOLOGY

1. Media History Project,
   "How Did Writing Start,"

University of Minnesota, http://www.mediahistory.umn.edu/archive/sumeria.html (Accessed April 20, 2011).

2. Mary Bellis, "Spacewar!: The First Computer Game Invented By Steve Russell," About.Com, http://inventors.about.com/library/weekly/aa090198.htm (Accessed April 20, 2011).

3. Mary Bellis, "The First Hobby and Home Computers Appeal: Apple I, Apple II, Commodore PET and TRS 80" About.Com http://inventors.about.com/library/weekly/aa121598.htm (Accessed April 20, 2011).

4. IBM Archives, "The Birth of the IBM PC," IBM, http://www-03.ibm.com/ibm/history/exhibits/pc25/pc25_birth.html (Accessed April 20, 2011).

5. Tim Berners-Lee, " Information Management: A Proposal," W3.org http://www.w3.org/History/1989/proposal.html (Accessed April 19, 2011).

6. Tim Berners-Lee, "HyperText and CERN," W3.org http://www.w3.org/Administration/HTandCERN.txt (Accessed April 19, 2011).

7. The National Research Council, "Realizing the Information Future: The Internet and Beyond," National Academies Press, http://www.nap.edu/openbook.php?record_id=4755&page=R1 (Accessed April 19, 2011).

8. Yahoo! Media Relations, "The History of Yahoo!: How It All Got Stared…" Yahoo.Com, http://docs.yahoo.com/info/misc/history.html (Accessed April 20, 2011).

9. Federal Networking Council, "Resolution: Definition of the 'Internet,'" National Coordination Office for Networking and Information Technology Research and Development, http://www.nitrd.gov/fnc/Internet_res.html (Accessed April 19, 2011).

10. Google History, Google, http://www.google.com/about/corporate/company/history.html (Accessed April 20, 2011).

11. Facebook Press Room, "Timeline," Facebook, http://www.facebook.com/press/info.php?timeline (Accessed April 20, 2011).

12. comScore Press Release, "comScore Releases March 2011 U.S. Search Engine Rankings," comScore.com, http://www.comscore.com/Press_Events/Press_Releases/2011/4/comScore_Releases_March_2011_U.S._Search_Engine_Rankings (Accessed April 20, 2011).

13. Cirian Giles, "Internet 'Right to be Forgotten' Debate Hits Spain," AP News Wire, April 20, 2011, http://old.news.yahoo.com/s/ap/20110420/ap_on_hi_te/eu_internet_right_to_be_forgotten_6 (Accessed July 1, 2011).

BIBLIOGRAPHY

17 United States Code §§ 107–122.

Abelson, Hal, Ken Ledeen, and Harry Lewis. *Blown to Bits: Your Life, Liberty and Happiness After the Digital Explosion.* Boston: Addison-Wesley Publishing, 2008.

Aristotle. *Metaphysics, Book I, Part 1,* translated by W.D. Ross, Internet Classics Archive. Available online. URL: http://classics.mit.edu/Aristotle/metaphysics.1.i.html. Accessed April 17, 2011.

Ars Technica. Available online. URL: http://arstechnica.com. Accessed April 16, 2011.

Arts and Letters Daily. Available online. URL: http://www.aldaily.com (Accessed April 16, 2011).

Bellis, Mary. "The History of Computers," About.com. Available online. URL: http://inventors.about.com/library/blcoindex.htm Accessed April 20, 2011

Comscore U.S. Search Engine Rankings. Available online. URL: http://www.comscore.com. Accessed April 20, 2011.

Dark, M. (ed.). *Information Assurance and Security Ethics in Complex Systems: Interdisciplinary Perspectives.* Hershey, Pa.: IGI Global, 2010.

FaceBook. Available online. URL: http://www.facebook.com. Accessed April 20, 2011.

Google. Available online. URL: http://www.google.com. Accessed April 20, 2011.

Google News. Available online. URL: http://news.google.com. Accessed April 16, 2011.

Health on the Net Foundation. Available online. URL: https://www.hon.ch. Accessed April 16, 2011.

Jelen, Andrew, Sarah McCord and Jennifer Pearson. "Information Infrastructure: Methods of Information Transfer in Nineteenth

Century Wisconsin." The Wisconsin Mosaic. Available online. URL: http://comminfo.rutgers.edu/~dalbello/FLVA/infrastructure/infoinfra/index.html Accessed April 20, 2011.

Libweb. Index of Libraries Worldwide. Ohio Library and Information Network. Available online. URL: http://lists.webjunction.org/libweb. Accessed April 16, 2011.

MasterBase Glossary of Technology Terms. Availble online. URL: www.en.masterbase.com/support/glossary.asp. Accessed March 20, 2011.

Media History Project. University of Minnesota. Available online. URL: http://www.mediahistory.umn.edu. Accessed April 20, 2011.

MedlinePlus. "Collection of Organizations Providing Health Information Arranged by Topic." Available online. URL: http://www.nlm.nih.gov/medlineplus/organizations/orgbytopic_a.html. Accessed April 16, 2011.

MedlinePlus. "Medline Plus: Trusted Health Information for You." Available online. URL: http://www.nlm.nih.gov/medlineplus . Accessed April 16, 2011.

National Coalition for Interfaith Media Justice. "2011 Media Fast Week: Where Do Your Values Come From?" Available online. URL: http://uccmediajustice.org/p/salsa/web/common/public/signup?signup_page_KEY=3193. Accessed April 18, 2011.

NetMarketShare, Analytics. Available online. URL: http://marketshare.hitslink.com. Accessed March 21, 2011.

RealClearPolitics. Available online. URL: http://www.realclearpolitics.com. Accessed April 16, 2011.

Slashdot. Available online. URL: http://slashdot.org. Accessed April 16, 2011.

The Internet Archive. Available online. URL: http://www.archive.org. Accessed April 18, 2011.

The Sheridan Libraries, Johns Hopkins University. Available online. URL: http://www.library.jhu.edu. Accessed April 16, 2011.

TrueKnowledge. Available online. URL: http://www.trueknowledge. com. Accessed March 21, 2011.

United States Federal Trade Commission. Available online. URL: http://www.ftc.gov. Accessed April 17, 2011.

University of California Library, University of California at Berkeley. Available online. URL: http://www.lib.berkeley.edu. Accessed April 16, 2011.

Wired Magazine. Available online. URL: http://www.wired.com. Accessed April 16, 2011.

Wolfram Alpha. Available online. URL: http://www.wolframalpha. com. Accessed March 21, 2011.

BOOKS

Hal Abelson, Ken Ledeen, and Harry Lewis, *Blown to Bits: Your Life, Liberty and Happiness After the Digital Explosion*. Boston: Addison-Wesley Publishing, 2008.

Mills, Steven, *Using the Internet for Active Teaching and Learning*. Upper Saddle River, N.J.: Prentice-Hall, 2005.

George E. Higgins, *Cybercrime: An Introduction to an Emerging Phenomenon*. New York: McGraw Hill Publishing, 2009.

ONLINE RESOURCES

American Library Association
http://www.ala.org/ala/mgrps/divs/yalsa/yalsamemonly/findgoodsites.pdf
"Finding Good Websites Online"

Connected Earth
http://www.connected-earth.com/index.htm
"Connected Earth: How Communication Shapes the World"

The Internet Society
http://www.isoc.org/internet/history/brief.shtml
"A Brief History of the Internet"

MedLine Plus
http://www.nlm.nih.gov/medlineplus/evaluatinghealth information.html
"Evaluating Health Information"

Teacher Tap
http://eduscapes.com/tap/topic32.htm
"Evaluating Online Resources"

The W3C Consortium

http://www.w3.org/History.html

"A Little History of the World Wide Web"

Yahoo! Media Relations

http://docs.yahoo.com/info/misc/history.html

"The History of Yahoo!: How It All Got Stared . . ."

● ● ● INDEX ● ● ●

Page numbers in *italics* indicate photos or illustrations.

buying and selling online, risks in *103*, 103–107. *See also* fraud

MICHAEL LOSAVIO is a Kentucky lawyer teaching in the Department of Computer Engineering and Computer Science and the Department of Justice Administration of the University of Louisville, Louisville, Kentucky.

ABOUT THE
● ● ● CONSULTING EDITOR ● ● ●

MARCUS K. ROGERS, PH.D., is the director of the Cyber Forensics Program in the department of computer and information technology at Purdue University, a former police officer, and the editor in chief of the *Journal of Digital Forensic Practice*. He has written, edited, and reviewed numerous articles and books on cybercrime. He is a professor, university faculty scholar, and research faculty member at the Center for Education and Research in Information Assurance and Security. He is also the international chair of the Law, Compliance and Investigation Domain of the Common Body of Knowledge (CBK) committee, chair of the Ethics Committee for the Digital and Multimedia Sciences section of the American Academy of Forensic Sciences, and chair of the Certification and Test Committee–Digital Forensics Certification Board. As a police officer he worked in the area of fraud and computer crime investigations. Dr. Rogers sits on the editorial board for several professional journals. He is also a member of various national and international committees focusing on digital forensic science and digital evidence. Dr. Rogers is the author of books, book chapters, and journal publications in the field of digital forensics and applied psychological analysis. His research interests include applied cyber-forensics, psychological digital crime scene analysis, cybercrime scene analysis, and cyberterrorism. He is a frequent speaker at international and national information assurance and security conferences, and guest lectures throughout the world.